"Influence isn't a score, it is the ability to cause, effect or change behavior. Phelps shows marketers how to add that 'little something extra' that influences consumer behavior and drives word of mouth."

- **Brian Solis**, Principal Analyst at Altimeter Group
Author of *The End of Business as Usual*, Named a Top 2011 Business Book by Publisher's Weekly

"*What's Your Purple Goldfish* is the new benchmark for customer service and experience excellence. The single source for numerous concepts and innovations that can help build the foundation for a world class brand! (I just hope my competition doesn't find this book.)"

- **Chris Zane**, Founder & President of Zane's Cycles
Author of *Reinventing the Wheel - The Science of Creating Lifetime Customers*

"Companies often benchmark their customer experience against competitors, leading them down the certain path to mediocrity. Stan's approach of delivering the unexpected, lagniappes, is a great way to break from the pack and instill a mindset of customer delight across your company."

- **Bruce Temkin**, Managing Partner, Temkin Group
Author of *The 6 Laws of Customer Experience*

"*What's Your Purple Goldfish* captures the essence of turning 'lookers' into customers. All of the real secrets of building a business are now out...thanks to Stan Phelps."

- **Stew Leonard**, Founder of Stew Leonard's
Author of *My Story*

i

"Your project has been an inspiration. I've talked about it many times, and included links in my articles. CEM can be complicated, but your examples show that with some creativity, companies can stand out by doing a little something extra."

- Bob Thompson
CEO of CustomerThink & Founder/Editor-in-Chief CustomerThink.com
The world's largest community dedicated to customer-centric business
Author of *CrowdService: Harnessing the Wisdom of Crowds*

"Painstakingly developed over years by Stan Phelps, a leading marketing practitioner, *What's Your Purple Goldfish* brings together strategies and tools that marketers need to succeed today."

- Bob Gilbreath
Author of *The Next Evolution of Marketing*

"*What's Your Purple Goldfish* busts a myth and reveals a simple truth about customer service. Stan uncovers the recipe for creating signature added value that increases customer satisfaction and drives positive word of mouth."

- Barry Moltz
Getting Small Business Unstuck at BarryMoltz.com
Author of *Bounce, Crazy* and *B-A-M*

"*What's Your Purple Goldfish* is unique in that it doesn't leave you asking 'Now what?' after you've read it. It's filled with actual illustrations of what successful businesses are doing right now to differentiate themselves and add value to their customers' experiences."

- Steve Curtin
Customer Enthusiast!, Steve Curtin LLC

"*What's Your Purple Goldfish* is a great guidebook full of real-world examples business owners can use to increase great experiences to delight and surprise their customers. Two years ago when I first heard of this program, I begged Stan to stop at 100 examples, thinking there was no way he could ever find 1,001 stories. True to the lessons in this book, Stan delivered this and then some, and this book is sure to inspire you to give your customers some lagniappe. Read this book before your competitors do or be left in the dust."

- **Phil Gerbyshak**, The Chief Connections Officer
Author / co-author of *10 Ways to Make it Great!* and *#Twitterworks*

"I have been a huge fan and contributor to The *Purple Goldfish Project* since inception because many companies talk about being 'customer centric' but few actually are. This project is a reflection of all those great companies that are getting it right every day, winning the hearts and minds of their customers, one customer at a time!"

- **Paul Dunay**, CMO of Networked Insights
Author of *Facebook Marketing for Dummies*

"At the heart of the marketing lagniappe concept lies the truth that we cannot simply meet the expectations of customers. Every experience starts with a person who had a need they would trade something of value to have solved. Lagniappe can create the difference between needs not solved or solved poorly, and needs solved so well we happily tell others of the experience. Purple Goldfish, crafted wisely in customer experiences, can be the difference between mediocre and great business performance."

- **Linda Ireland**, Partner at Aveus
Author of *Domino: How CX Can Tip Everything In Your Business Toward Better Financial Performance*

"In an industry that relies on part inspiration and part perspiration, Stan Phelps delivers an inspiring piece on customer experience that will surely help marketers to craft their own best-in-class practices. Stan leads by example, and as a result motivates the reader to get to work re-creating their own brand experience."

- **Jim Joseph**, President at Lippe Taylor
Professor at NYU
Author of *The Experience Effect*

"The reality is that your competition is probably delivering a very similar product or service as your company. In order to separate your brand from the pack you have to provide extra value to punctuate the customer experience. The funny thing is that going beyond a customer's expectation is not very difficult. Stan's concept of marketing lagniappe in *What's Your Purple Goldfish* nails the principle and proves that 'tying the bow' is just as important as the gift. If your organization delivers beyond its product or service, that will motivate customers to share their positive experience with others. When you can cultivate customers to become custodians of your brand you will beat out your competitors and grow revenues."

- **Lou Imbriano**, Former CMO of the New England Patriots, CEO at TrinityOne
Professor at Boston College
Author of *Winning the Customer: Turn Customers into Fans and Get Them to Spend More*

"The concept of lagniappe is as old as the baker's dozen - and just as rare in business today! If you read just one book on customer experience all year, make it Stan Phelps' *What's Your Purple Goldfish*. From its pages you and your staff will encounter countless examples of customer delight - well over the promised 1,001! If that isn't lagniappe, I don't know what is."

- **Ted Coiné**
Business Heretic and Un-CEO
Author of *Five-Star Customer Service* and *Spoil 'Em Rotten!*
Currently writing *Catalyst*

"Ever wonder how so many $90,000 sports cars get sold by virtue of an $8 T-shirt – often size "child's small?" Now you know. Stan Phelps' *What's Your Purple Goldfish?* compiles more examples of the decision trigger of reciprocity than I'm sure have ever been compiled in the civilized world. And, true to form, he throws in a bit of *lagniappe* here and there for the reader, too. Have fun! You'll get more than you expected!"

- Stephen Denny
President, Denny Marketing
Author of *Killing Giants: 10 Strategies to Topple the Goliath In Your Industry*

WHAT'S YOUR
PURPLE GOLDFISH

_____

How to Win Customers & Influence Word of Mouth

This book is dedicated to my beautiful wife Jenn

and our two boys, Thomas and James.

Their support and love made

the Purple Goldfish Project possible.

Published by 9 INCH MARKETING, LLC
Norwalk, Connecticut

Copy Editing by Jennifer Phelps and the 1 and only 'Keith Green'.

ISBN: 978-0-9849838-0-3
1. Business. 2. Marketing 3. Customer Experience 4. Word of Mouth

First Printing: 2012
Printed in the United States of America

What's Your Purple Goldfish? is available for special promotions and premiums. For details call +1.203.847.9340 or e-mail stan@9inchmarketing.com.

TABLE OF CONTENTS

PART I:

WHAT IS A PURPLE GOLDFISH?

Tall Tales from NYC - Choose Your Path Wisely - Shareholders vs. Customers

Thank You Groupon - Pareto Principle - Revolving Door Effect

Goldfish on the Brain - Mardi Gras, Seth Godin & Guppy Love Difference Between a Purple Cow & a Purple Goldfish - Purple Goldfish Strategy

What is Lagniappe? - Enter Samuel Langhorne Clemens - Acts of Kindness - Think of It as a Curly Fry - Plussing

Exploring the Ideas of Surplus and Status - Can Marketing Lagniappe Live in the Middle - It's More Than a Cookie - Greetings and Gifting

PART II:

THE 5 INGREDIENTS OR R.U.L.E.S OF A PURPLE GOLDFISH

PART III:

12 TYPES OF PURPLE GOLDFISH

Foreword

Have you ever met someone and within minutes of your first contact, you knew that you were kindred spirits? That's how I felt when Stan first reached out to introduce himself.

We first met a few years back when he was a brand new blogger. But I knew in an instant that he wasn't brand new to marketing. He got it. Like most people will never get it – Stan got the secret to marketing success.

He understood that marketing is about being so remarkable that people can't help but talk about you. That if you absolutely delight someone – they will not only come back but they'll bring friends. They become your sales force.

Stan delivers this marketing truth over and over again in this book all wrapped in the idea of lagniappe. What's so awesome about the whole notion of marketing lagniappe is that it not only teaches us what to do but more importantly, it reminds us that it must be done from the heart.

True lagniappe can't be faked or forced. We banter the word authentic around too much these days. But for lagniappe to work, it must be just that -- real and offered without expectation of anything in return.

In other words – you do it because you want to, not because it's in a marketing plan document or because your ROI calculator told you it would generate a 42.36% return. (And no…there's no such thing as an ROI calculator!)

As you read the stories that Stan has collected for this book, I think you're going to be amazed at the creativity and generosity that many businesses have and in the end, I suspect you'll be inspired to let your inner spirit of lagniappe loose.

You'll probably fill up a notepad with ideas of how you could do a little something extra to enchant your customers. When you've turned that corner and are thinking about them rather than what's in it for you – you're truly ready to practice lagniappe.

I honestly believe that the guys in the white hats do win in the end. And companies that embrace the belief that if you give first and you give generously – you will earn customers for life are marketing's good guys. This book shows us time and time again how to make that happen.

In the end, this book is Stan's own lagniappe for all of us. A genuine gesture of sharing what he truly believes with the hope that it is of great value to us. I'm so happy for you that you've found Stan, his book and are about to receive a gift that could, if you let it, change how you do business forever.

Enjoy!
Drew

- **Drew McLellan**
Top Dog, McLellan Marketing Group
Author of *99.3 Random Acts of Marketing*

Introduction

"There is a place in the world for any business that
takes care of its customers - after the sale."
– Harvey Mackay

What's Your Purple Goldfish? is not your ordinary business book. It aims to change the paradigm of how we fundamentally go about marketing our products and services.

Let's face it... we've lost focus in our marketing. We've been so laser focused on prospective customers that we've forgotten to deliver an exceptional customer experience once they've walked through the door. Advertising is no longer the answer. Traditional media is fragmented and for the most part ineffective. Customer support is non-existent, we're too busy outsourcing it to India. We've developed complex loyalty programs that confuse customers and only promise future benefits. What we really need is a concept that promotes retention and generates word of mouth at the time of purchase. That concept is called "marketing lagniappe."

Turning back the clock

I was first introduced to the concept of lagniappe (pronounced lan-yap) back in 2003 when I was part of a group called *"on the edge."* The group consisted of five guys that would meet every couple of weeks to discuss life and our pursuit of pushing boundaries to stay... *"on the edge."* I can distinctly remember the night fellow member Gene Seidman introduced the word. Gene explained that lagniappe was the practice of the merchant giving "a little something extra" at the time of purchase. He further relayed that in Louisiana the word is part of the vernacular and they have extended the meaning to any time someone goes above and beyond.

It was one of those rare things that just clicked when I heard it. Over the next five years I would share the concept with friends and subconsciously I began looking for examples in the world of

3

marketing. What I found was that very few businesses understood the concept of going above and beyond by giving that little unexpected extra.

Enter Norwalk, Stew's and Ritchie

The same year I heard about lagniappe was the year I moved from living overseas in Amsterdam to Connecticut. Our house is just up the hill from the most profitable grocery store in the US per square foot, according to the *Guinness Book of World Records*. Stew Leonard's was founded by its namesake in 1969. If there is one place I've been that gets the concept of marketing lagniappe... it's Stew Leonard's. We'll visit Stew's a couple of times in the book.

The house we bought in Norwalk is a beautiful old stone colonial that we refer to as "Het Stenin Haus" (Dutch for the stone house). Did I mention the house was charming and old? In the first five years we renovated the kitchen, upgraded the bathrooms, replaced the windows, overhauled the sleeping porch, landscaped the backyard and refinished the attic. The first project was the kitchen. A total gut and rebuild. Our contractor Brian hired a helper to patch and paint as the job was concluding. He referred to himself as Ritchie. Ritchie moved over with his family from Bosnia about 10 years ago. Ritchie was a quiet nice guy with an engaging smile. Even though he was doing a small finishing job you could tell he took great pride in his work. Ritchie's true specialty was taping.

One day I came home and found Ritchie patching a crack in the ceiling of our back hallway, which is next to the kitchen. I was a little taken back and at first a little defensive. This wasn't part of the job and I saw a bill coming. Ritchie just smiled and said not to worry as he was doing it for free. He saw that it needed to be fixed and had some extra material. That made quite an impression. Guess who was top of mind when we had our next painting project? We developed a long term relationship with Ritchie. Over the next three years we would engage him on almost every project in our house. Each time he exceeded our expectations and did a little something extra. Ritchie turned a couple hundred dollar job into tens of thousands of dollars of work.

The Longest and Hardest 9" in Marketing

In 2008 I launched a blog called 9 INCH MARKETING. Nothing personal with the title I assure you. Nine inches is the average distance between the brain and the heart. I refer to those nine inches as the *"longest and hardest"* for any marketer, given the goal of winning the heart of your customer. My first dedicated post was about the concept of lagniappe {Endnote 1}. With each post I included a small section called "Today's Lagniappe" with a fun extra bit of trivia, a joke or a story. My first guest post on another blog, Drew McLellan's *"Drew's Marketing Minute,"*{Endnote 2} was about the concept of lagniappe. My first Slideshare presentation {Endnote 3} was also about the concept of lagniappe. Can you see where I'm going here?

In September 2009 I wrote a post highlighting Wells Fargo and a concept called marketing lagniappe {Endnote 4}. That post would be the spark plug that ignited my passion and became the impetus for starting the Purple Goldfish Project {Endnote 5}.

Here is an excerpt from the original post:

9 INCH AXIOM – Little things

"Sometimes the littlest things can make a big difference"

Andrew was telling a story about how he was using the drive-thru at his local Wells Fargo bank. At the end of the transaction the teller asked him if he would like a sucker. Andrew was perplexed until he realized it was an offer for a lollipop. He drove away with a smile on his face. That lollipop was a small token or "marketing lagniappe" from Wells Fargo. It's a practice that goes a long way towards increasing customer satisfaction, especially when it is unexpected.

80% Rule – Wells Fargo understands the importance of servicing the needs of their current customers to fuel growth. Here is a quote about cross-selling from their website: {Endnote 6}

The more you sell customers, the more you know about them. The more you know about them, the easier it is to sell them more products. The more products customers have with you, the better value they receive and the more loyal they are. The longer they stay with you, the more opportunities you have to meet even more of their financial needs. The more you sell them, the higher the profit because the added cost of selling another product to an existing customer is often only about ten percent of the cost of selling that same product to a new customer.

That last sentence deserves repeating. **IT COSTS 10 TIMES MORE TO ACQUIRE A NEW CUSTOMER THAN IT TAKES TO UP-SELL A CURRENT ONE**. Nearly eighty percent of Wells Fargo revenue growth comes from selling more products to existing customers. The average Wells Fargo customer carries over five products which is more than twice the industry average.

Their focus on serving existing customers has two tremendous benefits:

1. It reduces attrition. Well Fargo loses less customers each year compared to its competitors.

2. It provides a competitive advantage against companies that only offer one or a few products.

A Project is Born

In late 2009 I launched the Purple Goldfish Project and started the blog Marketing Lagniappe {Endnote 7}. The project was an ambitious attempt to crowd source 1,001 examples of marketing lagniappe. Early in 2010 I started a video podcast {Endnote 8} with Jack Campisi. The ball was rolling. My friend Doug Pirnie once told me that everyone has a book inside of them. If that is the case, this one has been bubbling inside of me for the last eight years. I'm glad to be finally letting it out. I hope you enjoy it and profit by it.

Prologue

"Real generosity toward the future lies in giving all to the present."
- Albert Camus

TWO STORIES OF MARKETING LAGNIAPPE

The first is the story of a boy from upstate New York named David McConnell. {Endnote 9} At the age of 16 David started to sell books door-to-door. When his fare was not well received, McConnell resorted to a little lagniappe. David would promise a free gift in exchange for being allowed to make a sales pitch. The *"little something extra"* was a complimentary vial of perfume. It was a signature extra as David concocted his original scent with the aid of a local pharmacist. McConnell soon learned his customers adored his perfume, yet remained indifferent to his books. Soon he would concentrate solely on cosmetics, starting a company called the California Perfume Company that would soon become Avon Cosmetics in 1886. Who knew the first Avon Lady was actually a boy? Today, despite competition from hundreds of American and foreign brand name cosmetics, Avon is #1 in sales nationwide, with Avon Ladies ringing doorbells coast to coast.

The second story is about a company founded by a social worker and a psychologist with a passion for good food and a commitment to healthy living. {Endnote 10} Without the capital to open a restaurant, Stacy Madison and Mark Andrus began serving healthy pita bread roll-up sandwiches in Boston's Financial District. Their lunch cart was popular and soon lines started to form around the block. To make waiting more palatable (literally), Stacy concocted a lagniappe for customers waiting in line. Each night they baked the leftover pita bread sprinkled with seasoning to create different flavored chips. The chips were a huge hit and soon Stacy's Pita Chip Company was born. Stacy's experienced rapid growth, doubling sales every year which led to a multimillion dollar acquisition by Frito Lay in 2005.

Preface

*"In marketing I've seen only one strategy that can't miss -
and that is to market to your best customers first,
your best prospects second and the rest of the world last."*
- John Romero

Marketing is changing...

One could make the assertion that marketing has changed more in
the last five years than it has in the previous 25. Power has shifted.
The consumer has a bigger voice and traditional "tell and sell"
marketing has taken it in the shorts.

Let's countdown the Top 10 ways:

10. Retention is becoming the new acquisition in marketing

It now costs up to **10** times the amount of money to acquire a new
customer than it does to keep a current one. {Endnote 11}

9. We heard it through the grapevine

90% of customers identify word of mouth as the best, most reliable
and trustworthy source about ideas and information on products or
services. {Endnote 12}

8. Zip it or Zap it?

86% of consumers skip TV ads. {Endnote 13}

7. There is always an alternative

Over 70% of consumers will abandon a brand because of a bad
customer experience. {Endnote 14} [Does that make the other 30%
masochists?]

6. Consumers don't know what they like...

They like what they know or what their friends know. According to McKinsey, <u>67%</u> of all consumer decisions are primarily influenced by word of mouth. {Endnote 15}

5. Pardon the Interruption

In the 1970's the average consumer was exposed to **500** to 2,000 messages a day. Today it ranges between 3,000 and **5**,000 per day.

4. Love is a battlefield, for customers and marketing

Survey says: <u>94% of business leaders</u> say customer experience is the new battlefield. Pat Benatar could not be reached for comment. {Endnote 16}

3. Forget the water cooler

Social has become a game changer. Today's satisfied customer tells 3 friends, a pissed off customer tells <u>3,000</u>. {Endnote 17}

2. Double the Pleasure in Marketing

Customers gained through word of mouth have **2** times <u>the lifetime value than regular customers</u>. They also bring in twice the number of referrals. {Endnote 18}

and the #1 reason marketing is changing...

1. Search is a game changer

Forget about your cross-town rival, your competition is now just **1** click away.

PART I:
WHAT IS A PURPLE GOLDFISH?

Chapter 1

The Biggest Myth in Marketing

"The search for meaningful distinction is
central to the marketing effort.
If marketing is about anything, it is about achieving
customer-getting distinction by differentiating
what you do and how you operate.
All else is derivative of that and only that."
-Theodore Levitt

TALL TALES FROM NYC

A few summers ago I was in New York City with a colleague. Brad and I were at a trendy rooftop bar. One of those places where a bottle of beer is $14. We were waiting to meet a few people before heading over to a networking event. I noticed a guy sitting on his own for over 15 minutes. It was obvious that he was waiting for someone. I decided to strike up a conversation about waiting by offering my standard line:

"Do you know that we spend 10% of our life waiting?"

We started talking about waiting and I stressed the importance of being on time. Right then this guy shook his head and said something I'll never forget:

"There is no such thing as being on time. Being on time is a fallacy. You either are early... or you are late. No one is ever on time. On time is a myth."

This was a complete paradigm shift for me. I immediately starting thinking about how this applies to marketing and meeting customer expectations. I've always thought that the idea of meeting expectations was a surefire recipe for losing business. It almost guarantees you will fall short. It's similar to playing prevent defense in football. Prevent defense only prevents you from doing one thing... winning.

This new paradigm has only made it clearer for me. Meeting expectations is the biggest myth in marketing. Santa Claus, the Tooth Fairy and Meeting Expectations. Kids cover your eyes and ears... they are all myths.

In business you either fall below expectations or you exceed them. There is no middle ground. It bears repeating:

"There is no such thing as meeting expectations."

In a world where 60-80% of customers describe their customer satisfaction as satisfied or very satisfied before going on to defect to other brands, {Endnote 19} "meeting expectations" is no longer an option.

CHOOSE YOUR PATH WISELY

There are two paths that diverge in the corporate woods. Many companies take the wide first path and are happy with just meeting expectations. Others consciously take the narrower and tougher road deciding to go above and beyond to do more than reasonably expected.

Seth Godin wrote about this in a post entitled "Once in a Lifetime." {Endnote 20} He touches on these two paths:

> This is perhaps the greatest marketing strategy struggle of our time: Should your product or service be very good, meet spec and be beyond reproach or... should it be a remarkable, memorable, over the top, a tell-your-friends event?
>
> The answer isn't obvious, and many organizations are really conflicted about this. Delta Airlines isn't trying to make your day. They're trying to get you from Atlanta to Salt Lake City, close to on time, less expensive than the other guy and hopefully without hassle. That's a win for them.

Most of the consumer businesses (restaurants, services, etc.) and virtually all of the business to business ventures I encounter, shoot for the first (meeting spec). They define spec and they work to achieve it. A few, from event organizers to investment advisors, work every single day to create over-the-top remarkable experiences. It's a lot of work, and it requires passion.

You can't be all things to all people. Your strategy defines which path you will take. Don't get caught in the mushy middle. It boils down to the simple issue of meeting expectations. If all you want to do is meet expectations, then you are setting yourself up to become a commodity. If you are not willing to differentiate yourself by creating valuable experiences or little touches that go "above and beyond" for your customer, you will languish in the sea of sameness. Choose your path... wisely.

To under-deliver or over-deliver, that is the question

In today's climate you need to stand out by answering two important questions:

1. *What makes you different?*

2. *Is that differentiator a signature element?*

Creating small unexpected extras can go a long way to increasing retention, promoting loyalty and generating positive word of mouth. Investing your marketing budget in current customers is the lowest hanging fruit in marketing. Focusing solely on prospects in the purchase funnel and neglecting actual customer experience is a recipe for disaster.

SHAREHOLDERS VS. CUSTOMERS - WHO COMES FIRST?

My friend Jarvis Cromwell of *Reputation Garage* recently asked an interesting question, "Why are corporations in business?" He proposed that there are two sides of the argument:

1. Milton Friedman's theory that the sole purpose of a corporation is to drive shareholder value.

> *"There is one and only one social responsibility of business,"* *Friedman wrote back in 1970, and that is to "engage in activities designed to increase profits."*{Endnote 21}

2. Theodore "Ted" Levitt's theory that companies are solely in the business of getting and keeping customers.

> *"Not so long ago companies assumed the purpose of a business is to make money. But that has proved as vacuous as saying the purpose of life is to eat... The purpose of a business is to create and keep a customer."* {Endnote 22}

So – what comes first? The customer or the bottom line?

The last 100 years have seen corporations solely focused on the bottom line. The approach has been win at all cost with little or no regard on external effects, collateral damage or customer experience. The problem is that only pursuing the bottom line can neglect the customer. This was outlined in an article from HBS by James Allen, Frederick Reicheld and Barney Hamilton {Endnote 23}:

> *Call it the dominance trap: The larger a company's market share, the greater the risk it will take its customers for granted. As the money flows in, management begins confusing customer profitability with customer loyalty, never realizing that the most lucrative buyers may also be the angriest and most alienated. Worse, traditional market research may lead the firm to view customers as statistics. Managers can become so focused on the data that they stop hearing the real voices of their customers.*

The entire premise of *What's Your Purple Goldfish?* is that the customer must come first. Customer experience should be priority Number One. Stop focusing on "the two in the bush" (prospects) and take care of "the one in your hand" (your customer).

Chapter 2

Value is the New Black

"Price is what you pay. Value is what you get."
- Warren Buffett

THANK YOU GROUPON

DEAL is no longer a bad four letter word. It's a badge.

Value is becoming the new black. In challenging economic times, the climate forces both brands and consumers towards a "value" model.

Consumers are expecting more value. According to the *Brand Keys Customer Loyalty Index*, {Endnote 24} successful brands are those that stand out because consumers think of them as valuable. They don't see the term value as synonymous for cheap.

Brand Keys analyzed consumer values, needs and expectations and offered the following trends:

1. Value is the new black: Consumer spending, even on sale items, will continue to be replaced by a reason-to-buy at all. This may spell trouble for brands with no authentic meaning, whether high-end or low.

2. Brand differentiation is brand value: The unique meaning of a brand will increase in importance as generic features continue to propagate in the brand landscape. Awareness as a meaningful market force has long been obsolete, and differentiation will be critical for sales and profitability.

3. Consumer expectations are growing: Brands are barely keeping up with consumer expectations now. Every day consumers adopt and devour the latest technologies and innovations, and hunger for more. Smarter marketers will identify and capitalize on unmet expectations. Those brands

17

that understand where the strongest expectations exist will be the brands that survive and prosper.

4. It's not just buzz: Conversation and community is increasingly important, and if consumers trust the community, they will extend trust to the brand. This means not just word of mouth, but the right word of mouth within the community. This has significant implications for the future of customer service.

5. Consumers talk with each other before talking with brands: Social networking and exchange of information outside of the brand space will increase. This – at least in theory – will mean more opportunities for brands to get involved in these spaces and meet customers where they are.

USING PARETO TO FLIP THE RATIO ON TRADITIONAL MARKETING

Vilfredo Federico Damaso Pareto was an Italian economist who made a famous observation in 1906. He stated:

> *"20% of the population in Italy owns 80% of the property."* {Endnote 25}

The rule was popularized in the early 1940's by Joseph Juran and is now commonly referred to as the 80/20 principle, i.e. 20% of your customers will account for 80% of your sales. Basically, 20% of your efforts will net 80% of your results.

Enter the Phelps 80/20 Corollary

If we subscribe to the principle that, "80% of your results is generated by 20% of your efforts," then I respectfully put forth the *Phelps Corollary*:

> *"80% of your efforts will net you 20% of the results."*

Traditional marketing (tell and sell broadcast advertising) is ineffective. According to the late legendary retailer Joseph Wanamaker,

> *"Half the money I spend on advertising is wasted... the problem is that I don't know which half."* {Endnote 26}

I believe 50% is an understatement and therefore I propose that for the vast majority of your marketing dollars spent on the traditional funnel (the 80%)... you receive one dollar worth of return for every four that you spend given the Phelps 80/20 Corollary.

The Revolving Door Effect

There is a huge flaw when focusing the majority of your marketing efforts on the traditional purchase funnel. That flaw is "The Revolving Door Effect." If the majority of your marketing is mainly focused on prospective customers, you may be able to add between 10% to 25% of new customers per year.

Wait a second... most companies would say, "Sign me up right now for an increase of 10% - 25% of customers per year." The problem is that most businesses have huge problems with retention. It may not be uncommon to lose 10 to 25% of the customer base in a given year. The net effect is that you might negate all of your gains and in essence create a revolving door by not taking care of your new and current customers.

The overwhelming traditional view of marketing is the process of acquiring prospective customers. Eighty to 90% of marketing budgets are aimed towards getting consumers into the purchase funnel. We've become so preoccupied with generating awareness and interest that we tend to forget about our most important asset, our current customers. We need to flip that ratio on traditional marketing. We need to heed Pareto's Law and determine the 20% of traditional marketing we are doing that is generating the strongest ROI. Once you've earmarked that vital 20%, it's time to put the remaining 80% to work by putting the focus squarely on current customers.

By putting the focus on your current customers, you can generate the following three benefits:

- Reduce attrition
- Increase satisfaction and loyalty
- Promote positive word of mouth

THE SEA OF SAMENESS

How do you stand out in a sea of sameness? What is your one signature differentiator in customer experience?

Instead of being a "me too," what is the one special thing your company does that is superior and distinctive in the eyes of our customers? What is that little something extra that is tangible, valuable and talkable?

What do you hang our hat on? How do you stand out from your competition?

> *What is your warm Chocolate Chip Cookie like DoubleTree?*
> *What is your "Bags Fly Free" value like Southwest Airlines?*
> *What is your free peanuts and bonus fries like Five Guys?*
> *What is your free shipping upgrade to overnight like Zappos?*
> *Where is your "penny arcade" in the lobby like TD Bank?*

What's Your Purple Goldfish?

Chapter 3

Why Purple and why a Goldfish?

*"The thing that makes something remarkable
isn't usually directly related
to the original purpose of the product or service.
It's the extra stuff, the stylish bonus,
the design or the remarkable service
or pricing that makes people talk about it
and spread the word."*

- Seth Godin

GOLDFISH ON THE BRAIN

OK – I'll be the first to admit it. I am oddly preoccupied with goldfish. Mainly because the average common goldfish is four inches, yet the largest in the world is almost five times that size! {Endnote 27}

Five Times Larger!!! Imagine walking down the street and bumping into someone 25 feet tall. How can there be such a disparity between your garden variety goldfish and their monster cousins? It turns out that the growth of the goldfish is determined by five factors. Part of my obsession is my firm belief that the growth of a product or service is similar to that of a goldfish.

Let's break down a purple goldfish into two parts:

First the goldfish
Why a goldfish? Because the growth of a goldfish (your product or service) is affected by five factors:

#1. Size of the Environment = The Market

GROWTH FACTOR: The size of the bowl or pond.

RULE OF THUMB: Direct correlation. The larger the bowl or pond, the larger the goldfish can grow. The smaller the market, the lesser the growth.

#2. Number of Goldfish = Competition

GROWTH FACTOR: The number of goldfish in the same bowl or pond.

RULE OF THUMB: Inverse correlation. The more goldfish, the less growth. The less competition, the more growth opportunity.

#3. The Quality of the Water = The Economy

GROWTH FACTOR: The clarity and amount of nutrients in the water.

RULE OF THUMB: Direct correlation. The better the quality, the larger the growth. The weaker the economy or capital markets, the more difficult it is too grow.

FACT: A MALNOURISHED GOLDFISH IN A CROWDED, CLOUDY ENVIRONMENT MAY ONLY GROW TO TWO INCHES / FIVE CENTIMETERS.

#4. How they're treated in the first 120 days of life = Start-up Phase / Launch

GROWTH FACTOR: The nourishment and treatment they receive as a fry (baby goldfish).

RULE OF THUMB: Direct correlation. The lower the quality of the food, water and treatment, the more the goldfish will be stunted for future growth. The stronger the leadership and capital as a start-up, the better the growth.

#5. Genetic Make-up = Differentiation

GROWTH FACTOR: The genetic make-up of the goldfish.

RULE OF THUMB: Direct correlation. The poorer the genes or the less differentiated, the less the goldfish can grow. The more differentiated the product or service from the competition, the better the chance for growth.

FACT: THE CURRENT *GUINNESS BOOK OF WORLD RECORDS* HOLDER FOR THE LARGEST GOLDFISH HAILS FROM THE NETHERLANDS AT A LENGTHY 19 INCHES / 50 CM. {Endnote 28} TO PUT IT IN PERSPECTIVE THAT'S ABOUT THE SIZE OF THE AVERAGE DOMESTIC CAT.

Which of the five factors can you control?

Let's assume you have an existing product or service and have been in business for more than six months. Do you have any control over the market, your competition or the economy? NO, NO and NO. The only thing you have control over is your business' genetic make-up or how you differentiate your product or service. In goldfish terms, how do you stand out in a sea of sameness. How can you make yourself PURPLE?

MARDI GRAS, SETH GODIN & GUPPY LOVE

Why Purple? The reasons for Purple are threefold:

#1. Lagniappe is *Creole* for "a little something extra." Purple is an ode to the birthplace of the word [New Orleans] and the colors of its most famous event [Mardi Gras].

The accepted story behind the original selection of the Mardi Gras colors {Endnote 29} originates from 1872 when the Grand Duke Alexis Romanoff of Russia visited New Orleans. It is said that the Grand Duke came to the city in pursuit of an actress named Lydia Thompson. During his stay, he was given the honor of selecting the official Mardi Gras colors by the Krewe of Rex. His selection of purple, green and gold would also later become the colors of the House of Romanoff.

The 1892 Rex Parade theme first gave meaning to the official Mardi Gras colors. Inspired by New Orleans and the traditional colors, purple was symbolic of justice, green was symbolic of faith and gold was symbolic of power. {Endnote 30}

Ode to Seth

#2. Purple in marketing represents differentiation. Seth Godin established purple as the color of differentiation in his seminal book, *Purple Cow* {Endnote 31} back in 2003. Seth outlines the why, what and how of becoming remarkable.

Seth sets up the premise of the book with a story: {Endnote 32}

> *"When my family and I were driving through France a few years ago, we were enchanted by the hundreds of storybook cows grazing on picturesque pastures right next to the highway. For dozens of kilometers, we all gazed out the window, marveling about how beautiful everything was. Then, within twenty minutes, we started ignoring the cows. The new cows were just like the old cows, and what was once amazing was now common. Worse than common. It was boring."*

He further defined where marketing is heading: {Endnote 33}

> *The old rule: Create safe, ordinary products and combine them with great marketing.*

> *The new rule: Create remarkable products that the right people seek out.*

The Difference Between a Purple Bovine and a Purple Goldfish

Think of a Purple Cow as your product. Your product needs to stand out and be remarkable. A Purple Goldfish on the other hand is the distinctive way that you deliver that Cow and the extra value you provide. It's difficult to make your product itself "remark"able.

I had the opportunity to comment on MarketingPilgrim.com to emphasize this exact point. Joe Hall wrote a post about cell phones and the importance of being memorable. {Endnote 34}

Joe made the following assertion:

> *"Why can't I get one shaped like a banana with pink and purple stripes? I want one that can also open a bottle of beer, or something else equally ridiculous. Seth Godin will tell you that your brand has to be remarkable. However, before your brand can be remarkable it has to be memorable. It has to stand out from the crowd. It has to make me want to know more."*

Here were the thoughts I shared:

> *Great points Joe. You absolutely need to be memorable. Stand out or perish. The difficulty in Seth Godin's PURPLE Cow principle is that you need to bake that remarkability into the product. That is extremely difficult. A phone is a phone. It would have to be really remarkable for you to overcome the friction (p.i.t.a. factor) associated with making a switch.*
>
> *However – let me offer another take on how to color that phone PURPLE. That is by creating a few PURPLE Goldfish. A purple goldfish is something a whole lot smaller than a cow and much easier to create. It's based on the concept of marketing lagniappe. Lan-what? Pronounced "Lan-yap," it's a Creole word that represents the little unexpected something extra thrown in by the merchant at the time of purchase. In Louisiana lagniappe is part of the vernacular and represents anytime someone goes "above and beyond."*
>
> *Do small "PURPLE" things make a big difference? Absolutely. Imagine if you asked that same friend for a recommendation and she started gushing about "Product X" because they did these little things that were unexpected and extra. It could be the customer service they received (think Zappos), a feature that they decided not to charge for (think Southwest and Bags Fly Free), or a "thank you" with*

free minutes if you spend "X" per month (think Stew Leonard's).

Guppy Love

#3. Kimpton Hotels is the final reason for purple and a goldfish. This example of lagniappe was a huge inspiration. Kimpton has a signature (Purple) Goldfish that's well... a fish and a keeper **[Purple Goldfish #109]**. Introduced at each Hotel Monaco in 2001, Guppy Love has become a signature element that has gained the chain national attention. The hotel offers guests the ability to adopt a temporary travel companion.

> The "Guppy Love" program is a fun extension of our pet-friendly nature as well as our emphasis on indulging the senses to heighten the travel experience, says Steve Pinetti, Senior Vice President of Sales & Marketing for Kimpton Hotels and Restaurants. "Everything about Hotel Monaco appeals directly to the senses, and 'Guppy Love' offers one more unique way to relax, indulge and promote health of mind, body and spirit in our home-away-from-home atmosphere."

Is it possible for a PURPLE GOLDFISH to become PURPLE GOLDFISH STRATEGY?

Let's compare it to the critically acclaimed model in the book *Blue Ocean Strategy*. According to authors Kim and Mauborgne: {Endnote 35}

> *Blue Ocean Strategy is based on the simultaneous pursuit of differentiation and low cost. It's goal is not to out-perform competition in the existing industry, but to create new market space or a blue ocean, thereby making the competition irrelevant. The opposite of blue ocean is red ocean. Characterized by competition and a crowded space, red ocean is bloody water.*

Is there a middle ground or better yet a middle ocean?

Purple Goldfish Strategy is differentiation by added value. Finding signature elements that help you stand out, improve customer experience, reduce attrition and drive positive word of mouth.

Illustration: Purple Goldfish Strategy floating between Red and Blue Ocean

RED OCEAN STRATEGY	PURPLE GOLDFISH STRATEGY	BLUE OCEAN STRATEGY
Compete in existing market space	Compete in existing market space, but stand out by G.L.U.E 'giving little unexpected extras'	Create uncontested market space
Beat the competition	Differentiate yourself from the competition	Make the competition irrelevant
Exploit existing demand	Exploit current customer base to reduce attrition, drive loyalty and promote word of mouth	Create and capture new demand
Make the value-cost trade-off	Break the transactional market economy mindset and add value to exceed expectations	Break the value-cost trade-off
Align the whole system of a company's activities with its strategic choice of differentiation or low cost	Align the whole system of a company's activities in pursuit of differentiation via added value	Align the whole system of a company's activities with its pursuit of differentiation and low cost

Red Ocean Strategy and Blue Ocean Strategy, Copyright 2010 Kim & Mauborgne I www.blueoceanstrategy.com

CUSTOMER EXPERIENCE IS MORE IMPORTANT THAN EVER

Here are three leading indicators:

1. The cost of customer acquisition continues to rise, making increasing retention the lowest hanging fruit in marketing.
2. Consumers now have a stronger voice given the emergence of social technologies like Blogs, Wiki's, Facebook, YouTube, Twitter, Foursquare, TripAdvisor and Yelp.
3. Competing solely on price can "commoditize" your product or service.

In a recent Temkin Group survey *The State Of Customer Experience Management,* {Endnote 36} 7% of respondents think that their company is a customer experience leader today. A bold 61% want to be their industry leader within three years. This reminds me of one of my favorite quotes:

> *"Everyone wants to go to heaven... but no one wants to pay the price."*

27

Chapter 4

A Little Something Extra

"We picked up one excellent word - a word worth
traveling to New Orleans to get;
a nice limber, expressive, handy word - lagniappe"
- Mark Twain

WHAT IF . . .

What if there was a simple marketing concept that moves the needle towards achieving differentiation, driving retention and stimulating word of mouth? What if your execution was 100% targeted, with zero waste and given with a personalized touch?

I believe the answer lies in focusing a greater percentage of your marketing budget on the customer, not the prospect. Deal with the one that is "in hand" rather than the two "in the bush" through a concept called lagniappe.

What is Lagniappe?

Lagniappe is a Creole word meaning *"the gift"* or *"to give more."* The practice originated in Louisiana in the 1840's whereby a merchant would give a customer a little something extra at the time of purchase. It is a signature personal touch by the business that creates goodwill and promotes word of mouth. According to Webster's: {Endnote 37}

LAGNIAPPE (lan'yəp, lăn-yăp') *Chiefly Southern Louisiana & Mississippi*

> 1. A small gift presented by a store owner to a customer with the customer's purchase.

> 2. An extra or unexpected gift or benefit. Also called *boot.*

> *Etymology: Creole < Fr la, the + Sp ñapa, lagniappe < Quechuan yapa. Interesting fact- Napa comes from yapa,*

which means "additional gift" in the South American Indian language, Quechua, from the verb yapay "to give more."

Enter Samuel Langhorne Clemens

According to Mark Twain in *Life on the Mississippi*: {Endnote 38}

> *We picked up one excellent word–a word worth traveling to New Orleans to get; a nice limber, expressive, handy word– "lagniappe."*
>
> *They pronounce it lanny-yap. It is Spanish–so they said. We discovered it at the head of a column of odds and ends in the [Times] Picayune [newspaper] the first day; heard twenty people use it the second; inquired what it meant the third; adopted it and got facility in swinging it the fourth. It has a restricted meaning, but I think the people spread it out a little when they choose. It is the equivalent of the thirteenth roll in a baker's dozen. It is something thrown in, gratis, for good measure.*
>
> *The custom originated in the Spanish quarter of the city. When a child or a servant buys something in a shop–or even the mayor or the governor, for aught I know–he finishes the operation by saying– 'Give me something for lagniappe.' The shopman always responds; gives the child a bit of licorice-root, gives the servant a cheap cigar or a spool of thread, gives the governor–I don't know what he gives the governor; support, likely.*

A **marketing lagniappe**, i.e. purple goldfish, is any time a business purposely goes above and beyond to provide a little something extra. It's a marketing investment back into your customer base. It's that unexpected surprise that's thrown in for good measure to achieve product differentiation, drive retention and promote word of mouth.

So – is it just a Baker's Dozen?

In order to understand a baker's dozen, we need to travel back to its origin in England. The concept dates back to the 13th century during the reign of Henry III. During this time there was a perceived need for regulations controlling quality, pricing and checking weights to avoid fraudulent activity. The Assize (Statute) of Bread and Ale {Endnote 39} was instituted to regulate the price, weight and quality of the bread and beer manufactured and sold in towns, villages and hamlets.

Baker's who were found to have shortchanged customers could be liable for severe punishment such as losing a hand with an axe. To guard against the punishment, the baker would give 13 for the price of 12, to be certain of not being known as a cheat.

The irony is that the statute deals with weight and not the quantity. The merchants created the "baker's dozen" to change perception. They understood that one of the 13 could be lost, eaten, burnt, or ruined in some way, leaving the customer with the original legal dozen.

A baker's dozen has become expected. Nowadays when we walk into a bakery and buy a dozen bagels, we expect the thirteenth on the house. Therefore it is not marketing lagniappe. Now if you provided a 14th bagel as part of the dozen... that would be a purple goldfish.

ACTS OF KINDNESS
Another way to think of lagniappe is as an act of kindness.

There are three "Acts of Kindness":

1. **Random Act of Kindness** - we've all seen this before. Good deeds or unexpected acts such as paying tolls, filling parking meters or buying gas for consumers. They are usually one-off, feel-good activations. A random act of kindness draws upon gift economy principles. Giving with no expectation of immediate return, except maybe for potential PR value.

2. **Branded Act of Kindness** – next level 2.0. Here the item given is usually tied closely with the brand and its positioning. It's less random, more planned and potentially a series of activations. This has the feel of a traditional marketing campaign. Many brands are moving in this direction. According to EVP / CMO Joe Tripodi {Endnote 40}, Coke is leaning more towards "expressions" than traditional "impressions." Less eyeballs and more emphasis on touches. What is an expression or a touch? It's a "Like" on Facebook, a video on YouTube, sharing a photo, a tweet on Twitter etc.

3. **Lagniappe Act of Kindness** – 3.0 stuff. Kindness imbedded into your brand. Giving little unexpected extras (**g.l.u.e**) as part of your product or service. This is rooted in the idea of 'added value' to the transaction. Not a one off or a campaign, but an everyday practice that's focused on customers of your brand. The beauty of creating a purple goldfish as a branded act of kindness is that there is no waste. You are giving that little extra to your current customers. You are preaching to the choir... the folks who are already in church on Sunday.

Here is an illustration that shows all three:

Branded Acts of Kindness: Evolving from tactic to campaign to brand differentiator

1.0 RANDOM	2.0 BRANDED	3.0 LAGNIAPPE
Unpromoted	Promoted	Unexpected / expected
Untargeted	Prospect + Customers	Customer focused
One off	Campaign	Everyday
Opportunistic	Planned	Ingrained
Relevant to the recipient	Relevant to the brand	Relevant to the brand + recipient
In the field	Near point of purchase	At point of purchase
PR focused	PR + Brand	PR + Brand + CX + WOM

Think of it as the Curly Fry

My friend Rick Liebling recently shared some insight on lagniappe. Here is a snippet from his post at rickliebling.com: {Endnote 41}

> It's a fantastic concept that explains how brands can benefit by giving consumers just a little bit extra (read about it here). As I was reading "My life," {Endnote 42} a blog by my friend Anastasia Wylie, she made reference, via a Jason Mraz song, to one of my all-time favorite lagniappes. Ever go to a fast food joint, order regular french fries, and get one curly fry in the bag? Man, I love that! It's such an incredibly small thing, it's an accident of location really (the regular fries are right next to the curly fries in the kitchen). But it makes you feel like you received something you weren't supposed to, that others didn't get, and that you wouldn't necessarily have asked for ("hey, could you throw one curly fry in there please?"), but once you get it, you are over-joyed. That's a lagniappe.

I love how Rick has summarized the feeling you get when you receive a lagniappe. The curly fry is that unexpected little extra.

PLUSSING: WALT UNDERSTOOD THE IMPORTANCE OF EXCEEDING EXPECTATIONS

I had the pleasure on meeting up with Rick Cerrone at a networking function. He shared a story about Walt Disney **[PG #537]** Rick mentioned the concept of "plussing" from a book by Pat Williams called, *How to Be Like Walt: Capturing the Disney Magic Every Day of Your Life*. {Endnote 43} Here is a superb summary of the concept by John Torre: {Endnote 44}

> *Normally, the word "plus" is a conjunction, but not in Walt's vocabulary. To Walt, "plus" was a verb—an action word— signifying the delivery of more than what his customers paid for or expected to receive.*

> *There are literally hundreds, if not thousands, of examples of Walt "plussing" his products. He constantly challenged his artists and Imagineers to see what was possible, and then take it a step further...and then a step beyond that. Why did he go to the trouble of making everything better when "good enough" would have sufficed? Because for Walt, nothing less than the best was acceptable when it bore his name and reputation, and he did whatever it took to give his guests more value than they expected to receive for their dollar.*

> *Perhaps one of the best examples of Walt's obsession for "plussing" comes from Disney historian Les Perkins' account of an incident that took place at Disneyland during the early years of the park. Walt had decided to hold a Christmas parade at the new park at a cost of $350,000. Walt's accountants approached him and besieged him to not spend money on an extravagant Christmas parade because the people would already be there. Nobody would complain, they reasoned, if they dispensed with the parade because nobody would be expecting it.*

> *Walt's reply to his accountants is classic: "That's just the point," he said. "We should do the parade precisely because no one's expecting it. Our goal at Disneyland is to always give the people more than they expect. As long as we keep surprising them, they'll keep coming back. But if they ever stop coming, it'll cost us ten times that much to get them to come back."*

Chapter 5

Powered by Gift Economy Principles

"There are two types of economies. In a commodity (or exchange) economy, status is accorded to those who have the most. In a gift economy, status is accorded to those who give the most to others."

- Lewis Hyde

EXPLORING THE IDEAS OF SURPLUS AND STATUS

I'm fascinated by a concept of a "gift economy" and how it relates to marketing lagniappe. So – what is a gift economy?

According to *Wikipedia*: {Endnote 45}

> *"In the social sciences, a gift economy (or gift culture) is a society where valuable goods and services are regularly given without any explicit agreement for immediate or future rewards. Ideally, simultaneous or recurring giving serves to circulate and redistribute valuables within the community."*

A gift economy is the opposite of a market economy. In a market economy there is an exact exchange of values (quid pro quo). It is my theory that there is a hybrid called the lagniappe economy that can sit between the two.

Can marketing lagniappe live in the middle?

Here is a great analysis from a post by Kevin von Duuglass-ittu of Tonner Doll on gift economies: {Endnote 46}

> *This does not mean that the Gift Economy... and the Market Economy of business are incompatible, not in the least. In fact many if not most of our business exchanges are grounded in Gift-based relationships whose "gift" nature we simply are unconscious of and just assume. If you develop a keen eye for the gift-giving environment, and think about all*

35

the things that gift-giving in those environments signal, 1. a surplus others want to attach themselves to, 2. a magnanimous respect for the relationship beyond all else, 3. a debt structure that is positive.

Let's examine each of the three through the lens of a lagniappe economy:

1. **Surplus** – the idea of surplus is grounded in giving extra or creating an inequality. Lagniappe comes from the Spanish "la napa" or the Quechan "yapay" both meaning "something that is added." Lagniappe is the practice by the business of throwing in little extras at the time of purchase.

2. **Respect** – The gift or little extra is about the respect for the relationship. It becomes a beacon,{Endnote 47} a sign that shows you care. It's a physical sign of goodwill and customer appreciation.

3. **Positive** – A debt structure that is positive. This speaks to exceeding expectations by giving extra. The idea of an equal exchange (market exchange) is a myth in marketing. You either exceed or fall short of customer expectations. Providing that extra value provides an inequality that is

positive. The positive effect leads to a sort of indebtedness or reciprocity on behalf of the customer.

The Benefit of Surplus is Status

As a business why would you want to incorporate gift economy principles into your market exchanges? I believe there are three distinct reasons and corresponding benefits of the status gained through marketing lagniappe:

1. **Positioning** – stand out from your competition. If everyone is providing x, the fact that you provide x + y (gift) differentiates your offering. Less than 30% of consumers buy on price. You want to tap into the 70+% who are looking for value and a strong customer experience.
   Benefit: Differentiation

2. **Loyalty** – giving the little extra (gift) enhances the customer experience. It creates a bond between the business and the customer. The benefits of that bond includes increased loyalty and ultimately patronage as a form of repayment.
   Benefit: Retention

3. **Reciprocity** – Part of giving extra is to create goodwill (inequality). That inequality is repaid by positive word of mouth or digital word of mouse. The best form of marketing is via positive word of mouth. By giving a signature extra (gift) you provide something for your customers to talk, tweet, blog, Yelp or Facebook about.
   Benefit: Referrals

CASE STUDY: THE POWER OF A CHOCOLATE CHIP COOKIE

Flour, eggs, butter, chocolate chips and...

I recently had a quick business lunch at the Port Chester Coach Diner in Port Chester, New York **[PG #543]**. Upon paying at the counter I noticed a bowl of miniature chocolate chip cookies.

Here is the recap of the experience from my colleague Tim Heath:

> *We were pleased with the rapid and attentive service and quality of food. I walked away from the table content; but you guessed it, I was seeking a little something more to satisfy my appetite. Much to our pleasure, there was a container of complimentary small chocolate chip cookies next to the cash register. My colleague and I looked at each other simultaneously with a smile. We both consumed two free cookies and we shared our pleasure with the owner who was observing our enthusiastic response to his offering. A pleasant ending to a fine lunch. I look forward to my next meal at the Port Chester Coach Diner.*

The chocolate chip cookie has been a thread throughout the Purple Goldfish Project. {Endnote 48} The very first submission from Tom Haidinger was the DoubleTree Chocolate Chip Cookie.

DoubleTree and their signature chocolate chip cookie was named so many times they own the distinction of being the first brand inducted into the Purple Goldfish Hall of Fame. {Endnote 49} The Hotel has built a reputation on a unique treat that keeps leisure and business travelers coming back for more: its legendary chocolate chip cookie presented to each guest at check-in. Their signature DoubleTree chocolate cookies are baked fresh daily providing a warm welcome and refreshing hospitality for travelers around the world.

Here are a few fun facts about the cookie {Endnote 50}:
- DoubleTree gives out approximately 30,000 chocolate chip cookies each day. That's more than ten million each year!
- DoubleTree began giving out chocolate chip cookies in the early 1980s, when many hotels across the country used them as treats for VIP's.
- In 1995, DoubleTree enlisted the services of Nashville based Christie Cookie Company to hold the brand's secret recipe, which ensures that the same, delicious cookie is delivered consistently at every DoubleTree hotel and resort.
- Every DoubleTree chocolate chip cookie is baked fresh daily at each hotel.

- Each cookie weighs more than 2 ounces and has an average of 20 chocolate chips.
- The Christie Cookie Company uses more than 580,000 pounds of chocolate chips each year for DoubleTree's cookies.
- In June 2002, DoubleTree presented its 100,000,000[th] cookie!
- To date, more than 200,000,000 cookies have been served to delighted guests and customers.
- More than a million chocolate chip cookies have been donated by DoubleTree hotels to celebrate and thank deserving members of the community from doctors and nurses to police and firefighters, as well as non-profit groups such as orphanages, food banks and homeless shelters.
- From the United Kingdom to Canada and Italy to China, the signature chocolate chip cookie welcome is now being presented to travelers at DoubleTree by Hilton hotel locations around the world.

DoubleTree was followed by Midwest Airlines [PG #142] and Fort Wayne International Airport {Endnote 51} [PG #176]. The trio has given away more than 250 million chocolate chip cookies collectively.

It begs the question... what's so special about a cookie?

DoubleTree offers an explanation right on the brown paper bag the cookie comes in. "Why a cookie?" the headline asks. "Cookies are warm, personal and inviting, much like our hotels and the staff here that serves you."

Quoted in an article by the NY Times {Endnote 52}, Erich Joachimsthaler, chief executive of Vivaldi Partners said,

> *"When consumers don't know how to judge the benefits or the differentiation of a product — I don't know the difference between Midwest and JetBlue and United — then a meaningless attribute like cookies can create meaningful differentiation... The giveaway creates buzz, it creates differentiation, it increases a purchase decision."*

I'm not sure if I agree with "meaningless," especially if that little extra is a signature element. I subscribe to the philosophy that Malcolm Gladwell offered in *The Tipping Point*, "The little things can make the biggest difference." {Endnote 53} The chocolate chip cookie is not just a chocolate chip cookie. It's much more than that.

GREETINGS AND GIFTING AS A ONE - TWO SALES PUNCH

A recent study in the International Journal of Marketing Studies {Endnote 54} has revealed that giving a gift before purchase could increase consumer spending by over 40%. Here is a synopsis of the article by authors Hershey H. Friedman and Ahmed Rahman:

> *An experiment was conducted in a restaurant to determine the effects of a small gift upon entry and greeting customers with a thank you for their patronage. Two types of gifts were used: a cup of yogurt and an inexpensive key chain. The authors found that providing a gift upon entry into a store had an impact on how much was spent, on the performance rating, and on how strongly the establishment would be recommended. This study did not find any differences between gifts: a gift of a cup of yogurt had the same impact as a key chain. **The difference in amount spent between the group that was not greeted or given a gift and the group that was greeted and given a cup of yogurt was 46.4%**, a considerable amount.*

The article discusses the underlying principle of reciprocity, the power of surprise and the importance of giving without an implicit expectation of return. The conclusions are very interesting:

> *This study demonstrates that there is value in greeting customers who enter a store. Customers who are not greeted will spend considerably less, will rate the store lower on performance, and will also be less likely to recommend the establishment. Providing a small gift upon entry into a store will have an impact on how much is*

spent, on the performance rating, and on how strongly the establishment will be recommended.

The value of a satisfied customer to a business is immense. One study showed that customers who are totally satisfied contribute 17 times more sales to a firm than customers who are somewhat dissatisfied and 2.6 times as much sales as customers who are somewhat satisfied (Whalley and Headon, 2001). If all it takes to improve attitudes of customers is an appreciatory comment and an occasional gift, then organizations should use this approach as part of their marketing communications strategies.

From Yogurt to Peanuts [PG #94]

One of the Purple Goldfish Project Hall of Famer's is Five Guys Burgers and Fries. Jerry Murrell and his eponymous five sons (Matt and Jim travel the country visiting stores; Chad oversees training, Ben selects the franchisees and Tyler runs the bakery) represent the principles of marketing lagniappe. Added value is baked into the model at Five Guys:

1. Free peanuts when you walk through the door
2. 15 free toppings for your burger or dog
3. An extra handful or two of bonus fries
4. Free refills for your soda or ice tea
5. Free of logos and excess décor

The free peanuts you can shell are my favorite. According to Todd at cheese-burger.net:

> *While you wait for your order to be prepared, there is a **mountain of peanuts** just inside the front door to munch on. Free peanuts have become the trademark "thing" that Five Guys is known for. I saw over fifty bags, 50 pounds apiece, waiting to be opened and devoured. They have signs at the door to serve as fair warning for folks with peanut allergies, and they're pretty strict about not letting*

41

you take any peanuts to go as a safety precaution. But it's a pretty cool thing: order your cheeseburger, scarf down a handful of salty, ballpark-style, still-in-the-shell peanuts.

By my rough calculation Five Guys gives away over two million pounds of peanuts per year. Do little things make a big difference? For a company that does little to no advertising, here is the mantra from founder Jerry Murrell: {Endnote 55}

"We figure our best salesman is our customer. Treat that person right, he'll walk out the door and sell for you. From the beginning, I wanted people to know that we put all our money into the food. That's why the décor is so simple — red and white tiles. We don't spend our money on décor. Or on guys in chicken suits. But we'll go overboard on food."

Chapter 6

All Impressions are NOT Created Equal

*"If you do build a great experience, customers
tell each other about that.
Word of mouth is very powerful."*

- Jeff Bezos

THE ENGINE BEHIND WORD OF MOUTH - THE V4 PRINCIPLE

I first came across the concept of the v4 principle over 10 years ago from a hilarious forum post at Sportbikes.net. {Endnote 56} Here's the sanitized version:

> *Think about your entire history of relationships… Every person you dated long term, short term, prison term, and every random hook-up in between. The vast majority of those relationships were with someone you met through a common friend. Very rarely do you find a couple who met randomly at a bar. Most couples met through a friend, a friend of a friend, or a relative. The reason most relationships begin this way is what I call the "v4 Principle." "v4" is short for "Vouch For" and it is this reason that the majority of people in America hook-up.*

> ***EXAMPLE:*** *Say you're out on a Friday night and you see a cute brunette at the bar. You approach her, make small talk, and attempt to pick her up. To you she's a hottie with dating potential. To her you're just another one of the drunken masses out there trying to score. Now take the same situation as before, but when you see her at the bar she is talking to your best friend's girlfriend. Now when you approach you're SOMEBODY as opposed to the NOBODY you were before. The girl at the bar has a reference point for you and your best friend's girlfriend is there to vouch for you: "Oh, that's Fred. He's Mike's best friend. They work together*

at the law firm. He's a real sweetie, and he's soo cute when he's drunk."

See how it works? You're the same drunken dude either way, but now you're perceived as charming. So, if friends are largely responsible for our hook-ups, how does one improve his odds? Simple, just use this handy dandy friendship reference guide that follows to determine who you should hang out with more and which friends to discard:

1. Married Friends – Don't have any. They only hang out with their miserably married couples and they constantly attempt to pull the rest of us into their pit of despair. There is nothing for you here.

2. Friends Who Work In The Service Industry – Hold on to these. People who work in restaurants, bars, retail, and the like tend to have a plethora of same aged single people to kick it with. They are laid back and don't work until noon, so they're always up for a night out. Also, all hostesses are easy.

3. Friends Who Do A Lot of Drugs – Keepers. Whether you do drugs or not is irrelevant. People who do a lot of drugs tend to hang out with other people who do a lot of drugs... and, chicks who do a lot of drugs tend to be easy.

4. Religious Friends – No! No! No! All of their friends are usually bible-thumpers as well, and meeting a group of hot Baptists is like going to your favorite bar without any money. You can look all you want, but you can't have anything.

5. Strippers – If you have any friends who are strippers you can contact me. Please let me know where you'll be this weekend...

On a more serious note, v4 or "vouch for" is also how the majority of purchase decisions are made. A reference point or recommendation by a friend is the strongest factor impacting purchase intent.

According to research by Keller Fay: {Endnote 57}

Personal experience with a product or service is the number one catalyst for recommendation, with 86% saying they recommend a brand or service based on first-hand experience. 60% of word of mouth (WOM) conversations include advice to buy, try or consider a brand. Fewer than one in ten conversations advise avoiding a brand.

It only makes sense to maximize the experience with your customer. Giving that little extra provides AMMO for your customers to relay their experiences.

THE POWER OF WOM

One of the frustrations I have with the measurement of marketing is that it is fundamentally flawed. It assumes that all impressions are created equal. There is no weight given to context and / or the delivery mechanism.

Let's have a look at advertising, sponsorship, PR and word of mouth:

Advertising is a one way dialogue that is inherently biased. It's unlikely that a company or brand is going to show you their warts. Ads are vested in trying to grab your attention via interruption. They sell "blue sky" by putting the product in the best light. Let's call the impressions via advertising **V1**.

Sponsorship plays on the interests of the consumer. The company or brand aligns themselves with a second party. They are still vying for your attention, but now they are engaging you at a point of passion. Sponsorship works on the idea of affinity or attribution. Let's call the impressions via sponsorship **V2**.

PR is the proactive process of managing the flow of information between the brand or company and its publics. It allows for exposure to the target audience via third party sources. Those sources are predominantly mainstream media. This third party authentication provides credibility to the message. The impressions gained at no cost through PR are much more valuable than those obtained by paid advertising. Let's call those PR impressions **V3**.

WOM or **Word of Mouth** is the act of consumers providing information to other consumers. This is the **V4** or vouch for principle. V4 means that the consumer is standing up for the product and giving personal assurances to its value. It's been around for thousands of years and remains one of the most powerful forms of promotion. It's a friend recommending a new restaurant or the latest movie. New social media tools like Facebook, Twitter and Google+ have elevated word of mouth (WOM) to a new level. Call it WOM 2.0 or WOM on steroids. V4 reminds me of the old shampoo commercial where they start to split the screen by saying, "She tells two people, then they tell two people and then they tell two people..." Soon the screen has hundreds of people on it. That's the magic of WOM.

You need to figure a way to get people to talk about and recommend your product. A small, unique and unexpected touch that provides fuel to the word of mouth fire.

ENTERING THE "STATUSPHERE"

What are you working on?   What are you doing? What's on your mind?

These are the respective questions asked by LinkedIn, Facebook and Twitter.

Brian Solis of Altimeter Group {Endnote 58} is a marketing thought leader who is constantly evaluating PR's role in the shifting marketing landscape. I absolutely have fallen in love with a term that Brian has coined. It's called the STATUSPHERE. {Endnote 59}

In Brian's words with my thoughts in BOLD:

> *"We're shifting into a rapid-fire culture that moves at Twitter time. Attention is a precious commodity and requires a personalized engagement strategy in order to consistently vie for it* **[How are you engaging your best marketing**

*resource - **YOUR CUSTOMER?**]. The laws of attraction and relationships management are driven by the ability to create compelling content and transparently connect it to the people whom you believe benefit. **[What is your distinctive PURPLE GOLDFISH and is it relevant to your customer?]***

*The Statusphere is the new ecosystem for sharing, discovering, and publishing updates and micro-sized content that reverberates throughout social networks and syndicated profiles, resulting in a formidable network effect of activity. It is the digital curation of relevant content that binds us contextually and through the statusphere we can connect directly to existing contacts, reach new people, and also forge new friendships through the friends of friends effect (FoFs) in the process. **[Getting into the status updates of your consumer exposes you to their vast network]***

Twitter, Facebook News Feeds and other micro communities that define the Statusphere, are driving action and determining the direction and course of individual attention.

So – what does this mean to me as a brand manager, CMO or a small business owner???

The statusphere (people updating their status on social networks) has become the new digital water cooler. It's increasingly how people are sharing content. It's how a vast majority of folks are getting their news. Your goal is to get your brand into that statusphere. How do you WOW your customer to the point that they want to share their experience? In the words of Francois Gosseaux, {Endnote 60}

The reason why exceptional service is the new competitive differentiator is not just because it's easier for competitors to catch up product-wise, but because the news about exceptional service travels fast in the networks that matter – peer and friend networks where the buying decisions are increasingly being made. When people recommend products to friends, colleagues, and acquaintances, they do not focus on the features, functions and benefits the way many marketers have been trained to do – they focus on the overall experience of adopting the solution, and the exceptional qualities of that "whole" offering. So if you are like most companies and operate in a market where it is really hard to differentiate based on the product alone, you've got to focus your attention on WOW service offerings.

ARE YOU CREATING PROsumers OR CONsumers?

What are your customers talking about after leaving your business, logging off your website or hanging up the phone?

John Ernsberger of Stella Service {Endnote 61} stated that roughly six out of every seven tweets he sees involving customer service are negative. I'm not sure of the sample size on his assessment as they (whoever *they* are) say that 48% of statistics are made up on the spot. Whether it's 70, 80 or 90 percent, I think it's a generally accepted fact that the overwhelming majority of tweets involving customer service are negative. This led me to the following question:

Based on their experience... Is your customer a CONsumer or a PROsumer?

Are you invoking Bonnie Raitt and her most famous song, "Let's Give Them Something to Talk About?" {Endnote 62}

Specifically:

- Who do we want talking?
- What do we want them saying?
- How can we add value?

Here is how marketing lagniappe addresses those issues:

- The best marketing is 1st person word of mouth, i.e. your customers
- Control the things you can control... how you treat your existing customers

- Deliver value with your product or service and exceed customer expectations
- Provide that little signature something extra... a purple goldfish

Using a little artistic license (apologies Bonnie) on the song lyrics:

> *Let's give them something to talk about*
> *A little purple goldfish as they wander out*
> *Let's give'em something to tweet, blog and Facebook about*

PART II:
THE 5 INGREDIENTS OR R.U.L.E.S OF A
PURPLE GOLDFISH

Chapter 7

First Ingredient: Relevancy

"Existence is no more than the precarious attainment
of relevance in an intensely mobile flux of past, present, and future."

- Susan Sontag

MAKING LAGNIAPPE IS LIKE MAKING JAMBALAYA

Have you ever made jambalaya? It's a bunch of different ingredients all thrown in together. The chef takes a look at what's lying around in the kitchen and throws it all into a pot. Let it stew with some spices thrown in and voila... you have a yourself a jambalaya or purple goldfish.

Here are the five main ingredients or if you are an acronym fan (like I am), the R.U.L.E.S

> **R**elevant – the item or benefit should be of value to the recipient.
>
> **U**nexpected – the extra benefit or gift should be a surprise. It is something thrown in for good measure.
>
> **L**imited – if it's a small token or gift, try to select something that's rare, hard to find or unique to your business.
>
> **E**xpression – many times it comes down to the gesture. It becomes more about "how" it is given, as opposed to what is given.
>
> **S**ticky – Is it memorable enough that the person will want to share their experience by telling a friend or a few hundred?

Keeping it relevant

The first rule and probably the most important ingredient for a purple goldfish is relevancy. If it's just a throw-in or SWAG (stuff we all get), it probably is not that relevant. It needs to be something that is valued by your customer.

Let's look at three examples:

1. The Overnight Test Drive: BMW [PG #150]

I was driving up to New Haven on I-95. I noticed an interesting billboard from BMW of Bridgeport {Endnote 63} that stated:

BMW wants YOU to take an overnight test drive

IMAGINE THAT – they are willing to give you *"the ultimate driving machine"* for an extended period. No driving around with the salesperson (I hate that by the way) and no more imagining what a BMW might look like parked in your driveway.

I've done a little research. There is probably a strong reason why they want you take the car. Here is an excerpt from a *JD Power survey*: {Endnote 64}

> *"When it comes to the test drive, most shoppers expect to be able to test drive the vehicle for an hour or more, with most premium brand shoppers expecting to test vehicles for five hours or more. Most shoppers also expect to be able to take the test drive on their own, without the salesperson accompanying them."*

Strong move from BMW of Bridgeport. Even if those who test drive don't buy... they are probably going to talk, tweet, post or blog about it.

2. Buy one Pint of Ice Cream TO GO... and Get Two Cones for the Road: Toy Boat [PG #144]

How about making a cone in the comfort of your home? Here is what Molly Holtman shared about Toy Boat:

> *"Toy Boat, a great dessert shop on Clement Street in San Francisco, throws in two complimentary ice cream cones (cake or sugar, your choice) when you purchase a pint of ice cream. It's kind of fun to eat ice cream in a cone at home. Plus, their rocky road and pumpkin ice cream is fantastic."*

This a thoughtful and simple complimentary touch from Toy Boat . . . dare I say *sweet genius*.

3. Free Cleaning for Life [PG #232]

One of the nice extras that Tiffany provides (in addition to the little blue box) involves free lifetime cleaning of your rings.

From the Tiffany.com site: {Endnote 65}:

> *"Tiffany offers complimentary cleaning to keep your ring as beautiful as it was the day you received it. An expert will check your stone's setting and give your ring a thorough cleaning."*

My wife and I will stop by once or twice a year and drop off our rings. Come back in an hour or two and they've given you a complimentary steam, buff and polish.

Chapter 8

Second Ingredient: Unexpected

"So what exactly is 'surprise and delight?'
It's when you give your customer something - that little gift
or 'extra mile' - that they didn't expect.
Surprise and delight is that small benevolent act that
shows that you put the customer first, and that
you're willing to make their experience special."

- Marc Schiller

WHAT THE HELL IS A SCHEMA?

Steve Knox of Tremor (a P&G agency) took me to school recently. He wrote an enlightened post in Ad Age entitled, "Why Effective Word of Mouth Disrupts Schemas." {Endnote 66} The premise of the article is how to leverage cognitive disruption to drive word of mouth. By doing something unexpected, you force people to talk about their experience.

First off let me admit I had no clue what a "schema" was. So here is my interpretation of the word:

> It turns out that our brain remains typically in a static state. It relies on developing cognitive schemas to figure out how the world works. It recognizes patterns and adapts behavior accordingly. It basically doesn't want to have to think. For example, every day you get into the car and you know instinctively to drive on the right side of the road. Fast forward and you're on a trip to the UK or Australia. The first time you drive on the left side it throws you for a loop. Its disruptive to your normal driving schema and it forces the brain to think, thereby it elicits discussion (i.e. word of mouth).

Steve provided some great examples in his article. My one favorite was for a new Secret deodorant that P&G was launching. The deodorant utilized a moisture activated ingredient which kicked in when you sweat. The brand understood that this could be positioned against a traditional schema, i.e. the more you workout, the more you sweat and the worse you smell. The tagline for the brand became, "The More You Move, the Better You Smell." A staggering 51,000 consumers posted comments on P&G's website about the product. {Endnote 67}

I started thinking how this idea of disruption applies to the concept of marketing lagniappe. The second ingredient in the lagniappe R.U.L.E.S is the concept of being **Unexpected**. It's that little something that's an unexpected extra at the time of purchase. It's the unexpected surprise and delight that triggers disruption of our schemas.

Let's face it... most companies fail to deliver an exceptional customer experience. It's only when a brand goes above and beyond do we get shocked. And what happens when we receive that unexpected lagniappe act of kindness? We tell our friends, we tweet it and we post to Facebook about it.

Let's look at a three examples:

1. The Power of an Unexpected Discount [PG #134]

I was at the Pepperidge Farm Factory store recently picking up a few things. There was a senior citizen standing in front of me in line buying a few items. Her total bill was $9.96. The clerk informed her that all purchases over ten dollars received a 20% discount and asked her if she'd like to pick out something else. Quickly she made a b-line to the Milano cookies (good choice by the way) which essentially were free once the discount was factored in. I could tell she left with a smile on her face and a bounce in her step.

Those Milano cookies were an unexpected surprise and I can almost guarantee you that she will recount that story a few times. Turns out the folks at Pepperidge Farm make purple goldfish both literally and figuratively.

2. An extra acknowledgement for a hotel guest [PG #57]

Jack Monson shared this story from a business trip to Minnesota:

A few years ago, I was traveling to the Twin Cities often and stayed several times at the same Courtyard By Marriott in the suburb of Eden Prairie since it was close to two clients' HQ's. By the third trip in a few weeks' time, I had a nice surprise waiting for me. I walked in after a cold and delayed trip from Chicago to see a big sign in the lobby saying "Welcome Jack Monson." The manager informed me that I was their guest of the week (or whatever the title was) and gave me a card for free breakfast in the morning. Not a huge thing, but guess where I continued to stay every time I had to travel to Minneapolis over the next year.

3. KLM does a little extra for their fans [PG #595]

Barry Dalton shared the following tweet:

"A Purple Goldfish to start your morning and creative social engagement by @KLM (cc @9inchmarketing) http://bit.ly/cDs5nt #custserv #cex #scrm"

Barry shared a story about the Dutch Airline KLM. Here is the backstory on the KLM program: {Endnote 68}

KLM gives small personal gifts at Schiphol Airport to customers who have indicated through social media that they fly with KLM. If you use the location based social networking site Foursquare or place a message on Twitter at @klmsurprise, indicating that you will fly with KLM that day, it may just happen that the KLMsurprise team finds you and surprises you.

As soon as someone checks in via Foursquare at Schiphol or another airport KLM flies to, KLM tries to contact him or her through the @klmsurprise account on Twitter. The message hints that KLM has a little surprise. Next the KLMsurprise team comes into action to quickly offer a surprising, personalized gift before the customer is on board.

Chapter 9

Third Ingredient: Limited

"America has believed that in differentiation, not in uniformity, lies the path of progress. It acted on this belief; it has advanced human happiness, and it has prospered."
- Louis Brandeis

SIGNATURE TOUCH

The third of the r.u.l.e.s is the concept of being limited. What does limited mean? If it's a small token or extra, it means selecting something unique to your business. Ideally you want it to be signature to your brand. Something rare, different or just plain hard to find elsewhere. A limited extra helps you differentiate your offerings, while providing insurance against being copied by competitors.

Let's look at four examples:

1. Apples and Prints [PG #37]

Gene Willis submitted this gem from the West Coast:

> *The Fillmore, a famous San Francisco music auditorium has hosted everyone from The Grateful Dead to Snoop Dogg. At the end of each show they hand out a limited number of music posters... free. Each poster has its own unique artwork, and the date of the show and artist. People collect the posters, and sometimes look forward to getting the poster as much as the show. Generations of posters are framed and make-up the walls. Also, when you enter the Fillmore, there is a bucket of free apples and someone who welcomes you to the Fillmore. No wonder it's one of the most loved places to see a band perform live.*

The posters and apples are brilliant. It scores high on the five ingredients/rules of marketing {Endnote 69} lagniappe, especially limited:

> R elevant – each is designed with the artist in mind

> U nexpected – the posters are handbills that are distinctive in size

> **L imited – a limited run creates that "one of a kind" special feel**

> E xpressive – the posters are handed out when the concert-goers leave as a keepsake

> S ticky – a collector item that folks share and talk about

2. Donut Holes and Milk Duds [PG #83]

There are reasons native Chicagoans and tourists alike consider Lou Mitchell's a must visit. From the donut holes and the milk duds while you wait to the double-yolk eggs that make every dish even more sinfully indulgent, Lou's knows how to do breakfast.

Located in the South Loop, the restaurant has been a Chicago institution since 1923, and decades later, they're still dishing out thick French toast, enormous platters of pancakes, fresh-baked pastries, and of course, those famous skillets. The extras are just as delectable. Lou's boasts pure maple syrup, fresh-squeezed orange juice and slabs of toast served with every omelet.

Be prepared to make some new friends — chances are good you'll be seated next to strangers at one of the lengthy tables. Even if you don't bond with fellow diners, the employees' perpetually friendly smiles — and *free Milk Duds for the ladies* — guarantee that you'll want to return soon.

3. This example packs a CHOP [PG #218]

A good friend Doug Pirnie shared his experience of staying at the Four Seasons and receiving a signature purple goldfish when checking out. In Doug's words:

> *"At the end of my stay at the Four Seasons in Singapore, they gave me my own personal 'chop' – a stamp with my own insignia on it. Chinese tradition is for all documents to be 'stamped' with the owner's/writer's/artist's chop. If I can find it, I'll send you a note with my chop!"*

The hand stamp (especially for a Westerner) is something rare and unique. The addition of personalization on the stamp by the hotel makes it special. Two thumbs up for the staff at the Four Seasons who leveraged Chinese heritage to give an sticky compelling gift with the CHOP.

4. Guatemalan Worry Dolls [PG #238]

Besito means "little kiss" in Spanish. It's also the name of an authentic Mexican restaurant based in Roslyn, New York. I met Lilliam Villafane De Giacomo and she waxed poetic about Besito. She spoke of the amazing food, but paid special attention to two added value items. At the end of the meal the restaurant hands out wrapped churros and little worry dolls.

The following excerpt from a New York Times review mentions the churros and worry dolls: {Endnote 70}

> *"The best dessert was the churros given gratis to every table. The warm, long spirals of fried dough rolled in cinnamon sugar were delivered in a white paper bag. Along with them we were given tiny worry dolls to be put under our pillows to take away worries. My only worry was the amount of delicious food I'd just eaten."*

Here is another review from slapphappe :{Endnote 71}

A fresh dish of chunky guacamole is created at your table side from perfectly ripened fruits in a molcajete, the authentic Mexican basalt lava version of a mortar and pestle. It was near perfect for my tastes. Even at twelve bucks a pop we occasionally have two bowls. Their beef enchilada, huevos rancheros and chicken enchilada in creamy tomitillo sauce are all very good. Service is excellent. At lunch today we were each sent home with a complimentary "worry doll" and a wrapped churros to go. Legend has it that Guatemalan children tell one worry to each doll when they go to bed at night then put the dolls under their pillow and in the morning the dolls will have taken their worries away.

Chapter 10

Fourth Ingredient: Expression

"The manner of giving is worth more than the gift."

- Pierre Corneille

The How of Marketing Lagniappe

The fourth of the r.u.l.e.s is expression. Expression speaks to *"how you give"* as opposed to *"what you give."* A purple goldfish is a beacon. It's a sign that shows you care. That little extra touch demonstrates that the customer matters.

Let's look a three examples:

1. Oh Steward... there is a dinosaur in my room [PG #64]

One of the signature elements of staying in a state room on a Carnival Cruise is the towel animals. Every night guests return to find one of the 40 different types of animals. A cruise favorite, the folks at a Carnival create about seven million a year. That's a lot of folding.

About five years ago Carnival released a book called, "Carnival Towel Creations." {Endnote 72} The 88 pages encompass a "how to" manual on towel animal making. Think it's easy? New stewards at Carnival spend 10 hours of formal training to master the art of the fold.

One of the things that I like about the towel animals is how Carnival has leveraged them across their various touch points. They've been the focus of advertising, PR, direct mail and online. These towel animals literally have "legs."

2. Belt Buckles and a Post-it note [PG #608]

This is taken from a post by Drew McLellan from Drew's Marketing Minute {Endnote 73}:

I am . . .

> *A frequent traveler*
> *A wee bit impatient*
> *All about efficiency*

So it shouldn't surprise you that I have my travel routine down to a science. I can pack for any trip in less than 10 minutes.
I own a TSA approved messenger bag so I don't have to take my laptop out when I go through security. I always wear slip on shoes. And I just ordered TSA approved belts so I can scoot through the scanner without having to re-belt.

When the belts from BeepFreeProducts arrived, I was pretty pumped to open the package. This was the final tweak to my travel ensemble. (I know... I can't help it. Don't judge me!) But when I dug past the packaging, I found more than the belts.

There was also a handwritten post it note thanking me for my order and saying that they'd included a couple extra belt buckles so I'd have some variety to choose from.

On a simple post it note. Nothing pre-printed, nothing fancy. Just a note from Jim.

It probably cost him 2 minutes to jot the note. But I felt the love. Why?

It was unexpected: This was my first order from the company so I had no real expectations. I hadn't spent a huge amount of money and they don't have a super sexy website, product etc. So I wasn't expecting the creativity and the personal touch.

It was personal: If it had been a pre-printed card, it probably wouldn't have been as memorable or noteworthy. He addressed the note to me, not "dear customer or sir." Whether it's true or not, I felt like Jim really did want me to have those extra buckles. He really cared that I could mix and match my buckles.

Many people believe that creating a lasting love affair with your customers is going to be incredibly expensive. It doesn't have to be. In fact, you can't buy their love. If you try too hard or it feels like you are throwing money at it, rather than throwing your heart into it, it will backfire. Instead of them feeling your love, they'll feel a little cheap, like you think they can be bought. But let Jim's post it note remind us all that it's the heart that counts, not the cost.

3. It's not about the Money

Examples from BMW [PG #190], Les Schwab Tires [PG #17] and The Four Seasons [PG #192]... Total Cost = $0

BMW of Darien [courtesy of Jack Sarsen]

When I dropped my car off for service, I had to move 2 car seats to the loaner. Upon my return, a service guy, obviously recognizing the number on the car, walks out to the loaner as soon as I parked and told me to hold tight. Within a minute my car pulled up and two service guys helped me make the car seat switch with my small children in tow. Another walked out and handed me my paperwork and said, "Thank you, have a nice day."

Les Schwab Tires [From Cody Goldberg]

"The service people jog to your car when you pull in to the service center."

Four Seasons Hotel [From Stephanie Hadden]

"When you check in, the front desk attendant will walk around to the front of the counter and hand you your key

while using your name and anticipating your every need. This customer service costs them nothing extra but makes you feel like a million bucks."

Marketing Takeaway: You don't have to tap into $$$ to go the extra mile. Being quick, responsive and alert with your customer service can make all the difference.

Chapter 11

Fifth Ingredient: Sticky

"Why wait to be memorable?"
-Tony Robbins

Sticking out in a Sea of Sameness?

The fifth of the r.u.l.e.**s** is sticky. You want something that sticks. A strong marketing lagniappe promotes word of mouth. Your purple goldfish needs to be memorable and talkable.

Two questions to ask yourself:

1. Is it water cooler material?

2. Will your customer tell three people or 3,000? {Endnote 74}

Let's looks at four examples:

1. Dropping the Sticky Bomb [PG #152]

On January 2nd (officially the laziest day of the Year), "The Make It Great Guy" Phil Gerbyshak dropped a bomb on me. A P-nut bomb to be exact.

I asked him if he had any examples of marketing lagniappe and he immediately posted this gem from Milwaukee. Phil nominated AJ Bombers. In Phil's words:

> *One of my favorite Purple Goldfish is AJ Bombers (@ajbombers) in Milwaukee. Joe [Sorge] and his team consistently provide the Purple Goldfish by offering free peanuts... shot at you in metal WWII bombers. It's way fun to get those from the bartenders. Making AJ Bombers even more fun is the fact he is on Twitter, recognizing customers and anyone who mentions the place, hosts Tweetups at Bombers, has guest bartenders where he donates shots folks can sell...with all proceeds going to the charity of the*

69

guest bartender's choice. Full disclosure: I've been a guest bartender and raised money for my charity. Last but not least is everyone who wants one can get a Sharpie and put their Twitter handle anywhere they want at AJ Bombers, so when friends come in, they can look for your Twitter name and leave you a tweet... in real life.

Do you believe in love at first sight? I do now. I'm a huge Five Guys fan because of the free peanuts. In fact – I put them in the Purple Goldfish Hall of Fame based on their peanuts and the handfuls of extra fries. AJ Bombers takes the P-nut to the next level! Move over "El Muchachos Cinco"... you've got some company. Of the five main ingredients or R.U.L.E.S, Bombers scores huge on stickiness. At AJ Bombers, the bartenders literally send bombers attached to rails above the bar to deliver the nuts. Joe e-mailed me and added an interesting wrinkle,

> *"By the way, not only do we offer free p-nuts to our guests while they are at the restaurant, they always get BONUS unexpected nuts with all 'to go' orders. Their reactions are priceless, they love it."*

Here is a rundown of the Top 5 from AJ Bombers:

1. **P-nut Bomber** – a signature way to deliver peanuts to the respective booths.
2. **Oversize Beach Chairs** – a couple larger than life beach chairs. You feel like a silly little kid while sitting (but isn't that the point).
3. **Quad Cow** – take on the quad cow at AJ Bombers. After you've swallowed the last bite of your four patty burger you can sign your name on the sacred cow that adorns the wall.
4. **Sharpies** – grab a marker and leave you name or Twitter handle on the wall. You are now part of AJ Bombers.
5. **Streamlined menu** – your menu is a narrow piece of paper that details the various burgers. Grab a pencil and start writing... choose wisely.

2. A handful of Goldfish... plus a real Purple Cow [PG #221]

Phil also shared another gem from Milwaukee,

> *I was just thinking about one of my favorite Milwaukee Purple Goldfish, Pizza Shuttle. From the original Andy Warhol "Purple Cow" in the dining area, to the fantastic hold messages, to the old Pizza Shuttle trading cards they let people collect of their drivers, to the fact you get free pizza on your birthday, to the in-store photo booth perfect for taking pictures, it's all fun. Couple that with late-night delivery of pizza AND frozen custard AND chicken AND burgers, fun, unique people who work there and you get an amazing place to eat and an experience for everyone. A few other wonderfully inventive things they do: The world's largest pizza, available for dine-in only; An amazing program where they give back HUGE to the community they serve; Delivery to all the colleges, hotels, and universities in the area; Employing nearly 100 people in a town that can desperately use it.*

I find that businesses that tend to get the concept of marketing lagniappe usually have multiple purple goldfish. They understand that in order to stand out you need to differentiate by giving those little unexpected extras. Pizza Shuttle is no exception.

Here is a summary of their Top 5:

1. **The Purple Cow** (hat tip to Seth) – How many pizza places have a framed Andy Warhol on display? Genius interplay of pop culture and a homage to the dairy state of Wisconsin.
2. **A Picture Booth** – Take your experience home with you with a branded strip of black and white photos. Great memento for a date with your squeeze or a night out with your friends. A picture may be worth a thousand pizzas.
3. **The Largest Pie in Wisconsin** – Be memorable by offering a $39.95 gut buster. According to an article by Jason McDowell {Endnote 75}, it looks like they throw in the ice cream as an added lagniappe.
4. **FREE WiFi** – This is becoming a no brainer as of late. But again – how many pizza places are offering you complimentary wireless access?
5. **Unique hold music** – Imagine wanting to be put on hold??? Smart move when you have a robust delivery business. Create some fun messages so people can be entertained while they wait.

3. Promoting Word of Mouth using spare change [PG #672]

A clean example taken from a post by Ben Popken at *"The Consumerist:"* {Endnote 76}

> *As a favor to guests, one hotel washes every coin it receives, just like it's done since 1938. The practice at the St. Francis Hotel in San Francisco is said to have started when hotelier Dan London observed that some coins sullied a woman's white gloves. At the time, coins were used for everything from tips to payphones to taxicabs. Back then washing the coins were a full-time job. Now it's only 10 hours a week, but the practice continues, passed down from one generation to the next.*
>
> *The coins are first passed from the general cashier to the coin washer who dumps them into a silver burnisher. Along with the coins, the burnisher is filled with water, buckshot to knock the dirt off, and a healthy pour of 20 Mule Team Borax*

soap. After three hours of swishing the coins around, Holsen uses a metal ice scoop to pour the loot into a perforated roast pan that sifts out the buckshot. The wet coins are then spread out on a table beneath heat lamps. This is where once-rusted copper pennies turn into shimmering bronze coins. Quarters look like sparkling silver bits.

Marketing Lagniappe Takeaway – Do guests of the St. Francis really care that their coins are sparkly? Other than the germophobes... probably not. But this purple goldfish ranks extremely high on sticky.

4. How do you overtake a luxury brand with the heritage of Mercedes-Benz?

While preparing to launch an unknown brand with no heritage against established European brands such as BMW and Mercedes, Japanese automaker Lexus set out to build the perfect car and retail experience. Nothing less than a "relentless pursuit of perfection" was the mandate when the brand was launched in 1989. Twenty three years later the brand is all grown up. It's kicking ass and taking nameplates. One of the ways that Lexus distinguishes itself is through its customer service and by doing the little talkable extras.

Ray Catena Lexus of Monmouth [New Jersey] treats each customer as they would a guest in their own home. It's as simple as making sure the coffee is always fresh, the loaner car is always clean, or just giving a friendly smile and hello when passing a customer in the showroom.

Here an 'F' is a A+ [PG #200]

1. FORE!!! When you drop your car off for service at Ray Catena Lexus, bring your golf clubs. You can practice your game at an indoor driving range and golf course simulator adjacent to the plush waiting lounge.

2. Follow Up - Dedicated to make sure your experience was perfect. Ray Catena has one person whose sole job is to call

73

people who have had warranty service to make sure everything went smoothly. According to an article at forbes.com, {Endnote 77}

> *"Customer surveys revealed that 99.2% of people who serviced their cars at the store would recommend it. That meant there were about a dozen less-than-perfect surveys out of 1,400. Those customers got personal letters and phone calls offering apologies."*

3. **Free Car Wash** – A staple of the Lexus service is the free car wash with your service. I was talking with Shelley Grosman, a co-worker who brings her car into Ray Catena for service. We discussed their service and she started gushing about how they are so committed and that everything is always done just right. When Shelley mentioned the car wash, I shared my feeling that the free car wash has become expected, kind of like the baker's dozen. It's loses a little bit of its specialness if everyone is doing it. Audi, BMW and VW have also been cited in the Project for the car wash. Shelley mentioned that on a recent trip that the wait for her car to be washed was long. Lexus apologized and handed her a voucher for a car wash down the street. Another time Lexus couldn't wash her car in lieu of the constant rain. Instead they filled her gas tank on the house.

PART III:
12 TYPES OF PURPLE GOLDFISH

Chapter 12

12 Types of Purple Goldfish

"There are no traffic jams along the extra mile."
- Roger Staubach

ARE YOU DOING THE LITTLE THINGS FOR YOUR CUSTOMERS?

Giving Little Unexpected Extras (GLUE) shows you care. There are a dozen different types of marketing lagniappe. Half are based on "value" and half are based on "maintenance" according to the value / maintenance matrix:

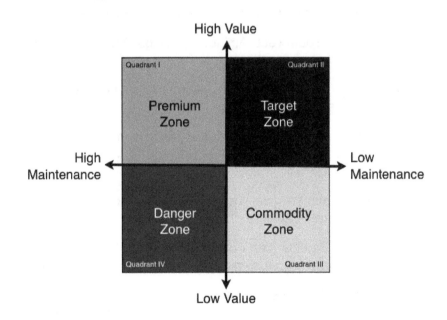

Here are the main elements of both:

Value (the what and when of customer experience)

- What are the tangible and intangible benefits that your service or product provides?
- Does your product or service go above and beyond to exceed customer expectations?
- Are you giving that little unexpected extra to surprise and delight your customer?

Maintenance (the who and how of customer experience)

- What is the buying experience like for your customer?
- Do you make things turnkey or simple for your customer?
- Are you responsive to problems / issues for your customer?

HERE ARE THE 12 CATEGORIES:

#1. **Throw-ins** (value) – little extras that are included with your product or service. They help you stand out in a sea of sameness:

> Example: Southwest Airlines – "Bags Fly Free" and no change fees on Southwest.

#2. **In the Bag / Out of the Box** (value) - little unexpected things that are added as a surprise.

> Example: Maggiano's - order a pasta dish and Maggiano's will pack an additional one up for you to take home on the house.

#3. **Sampling** (value) - give your customer an additional taste by offering a free something extra on the house.

> Example: Bigelow Tea - order a box of tea from Bigelow and you'll be treated to a sample of another flavor on the house.

#4. **First & Last Impressions** (value) - you have two chances to make an impression. When your customer comes through the door and right before they walk out, hang up or log off. These little extras make you memorable and more importantly talkable.

Example: Hard Rock - When you check in the Hard Rock will let you sample a Gibson guitar. Check in, plug-in and rock out.

#5. **Guarantees** (value) - giving your customers that little extra pledge that you'll stand behind your product or service.

Example: L.L. Bean - Leon Leonwood backs his product... for a lifetime.

#6. **Pay it Forward** (value) - give a little extra back to the community.

Example: Plaza Cleaners - if you are out of work and need a suit cleaned for an interview, Plaza will clean it for free.

#7. **Follow-up call** (maintenance) - make the little extra follow up with your customer.

Example: Rite Aid follows up with a call to check on a patient.

#8. **Added Service** (maintenance) - the little extra that's an added unexpected service.

Example: Safelite repairs or replaces your glass, but they also vacuum your car and clean your windows.

#9. **Convenience** (maintenance) - the little extras you add to make things easier for your customers.

Example: Amazon - Frustration free packaging that's hassle free and good for the environment.

#10. **Waiting** (maintenance) - all customers hate to wait. If its inevitable, how can you do a little extra to make it more bearable.

Example: Pacific Cafe - while you wait for your table, enjoy a glass of wine on the house.

#11. **Special Needs** (maintenance) - acknowledging that some customers have needs that require special attention.

> Example: Rainforest Cafe - the restaurant caters to the needs of customer by doing a little extra for those with food allergies.

#12. **Handling Mistakes** (maintenance) - admitting that you're wrong and doing the little extra above and beyond to make it more than right.

> Example: Nurse Next Door - this nursing agency in Canada takes the idea of "humble pie" to heart, literally delivering a pie when they make a mistake.

Chapter 13

#1 - Throw-ins

"A fellow who does things that count,
doesn't usually stop to count them."

- Variation of a saying by Albert Einstein

The next six chapters in the book will cover the types of purple goldfish associated with "VALUE":

Throw-ins are the little unexpected extras that are included with your product or service.

The lowest hanging fruit in marketing lagniappe is added value.

Let's look at seventeen examples:

1. A BOWLFUL OF QUARTERS [PG #460]

The etymology of Lagniappe stems from the Quechan *"yapay"* {Endnote 78} which means "to give more." Zane's lives by this mantra, leveraging customer service as point of differentiation. A 30+ year veteran of the retail bicycle industry, Chris Zane has built Zane's Cycles of Branford, Connecticut into one of the largest bicycle stores in the nation by giving customers more than they expect. More importantly they stand behind the sale by giving more service than is reasonably expected (especially by competitors).

Zane's is willing to spend $100 to service a customer. To illustrate the point Chris uses the metaphor of a bowl filled with 400 quarters. During presentations he walks around with a bowl and encourages members of the audience to take quarters. Most take a few quarters, but no one ever takes the whole bowl. According to Chris:

"The point is that when you as a customer are presented with more than what seems reasonable, like a bowl of 400 quarters, you will self-regulate. By providing more service than what folks consider reasonable, we can build trust and loyalty and remind them how hard we're working on their behalf."

Here are some of the compelling ways that Zane's offers little extras to maximize lifetime value:

1. **Free Trade-In Program for Kids** - buy a bike for your child at Zane's. When they outgrow it, simply bring it back to trade-up. Zane's gives you a credit for the price of the former bike towards a new one.
2. **Gift Certificates in Water Bottles** - Buy a gift certificate and Zane's will throw in a complimentary branded water bottle that holds the certificate.
3. **The One Dollar Rule** - Zane's doesn't charge for any parts that cost them one dollar or less. Need a master link for your chain? It's on the house. In fact they typically will throw in an extra master link for lagniappe.
4. **Coffee Bar** - Zane's has a nice espresso bar in the store encouraging customers to sit down, relax and enjoy a cup of gourmet coffee.
5. **Set of Small Tools** - Zane's provides a complimentary toolkit when shipping bikes to premium recipients.
6. **Webcam** - Zane's has a camera in the repair shop which gives customers the ability to Skype the team.
7. **Personal Notes** - each person who buys a bike receives a handwritten thank you note
8. **Test Rides** - Want to test a bike at Zane's? You're free to take it out for a ride. No credit card or drivers license required. Each year they lose a handful of bikes, but the small cost is insignificant compared to the trust gained and hassle avoided.

2. You are FREE to change your travel plans [PG #670]

Southwest Airlines stands for "freedom" in air travel. Following up on the successful Bags Fly Free {Endnote 79} program, Southwest introduces the next chapter in eliminating fees:

> *"No charge for change fees at Southwest. Saving customers upwards of $150."*

At Southwest fees are a four letter word, a very bad four letter word. Here is a rundown of how they treat fees:

- No 1st or 2nd Checked Bag Fees
- No Change Fees
- No Fuel Surcharge Fees
- No Snack Fees
- No Aisle or Window Seat Fees
- No Curbside Check in Fees
- No Phone Reservation Fees

Marketing Lagniappe Takeaway: Fees don't fly at Southwest. Sometimes marketing lagniappe is not about what you give, but rather what you decide not to charge for.

3. Channel your inner Robin Hood... give it a shot in Lana'i [PG #730]

A bow and arrow aren't just tools for William Tell. At Four Seasons Resort Lana'i in Hawaii, you are invited to try your hand at archery or clay shooting for a chance to win a prestigious crystal pineapple.

Here's a review from *Trip Advisor*: {Endnote 80}

> *"My son and I enjoyed going to the shooting range and taking a lesson with the air rifle, followed by target practice and each of us winning a crystal pineapple for our accuracy during the shooting contest. The instructor, Reno, was very friendly and made the experience memorable for us."*

4. A Jelly Bean and Huge Scoops [PG #333]

Wilson's courtesy of Jody Padar:

> *At my favorite ice cream store in Door County, Wisconsin, they put a jelly bean at the bottom of the ice cream cone so it doesn't drip. They also give the biggest scoop ever. It's tradition. The girls who scoop the ice cream live upstairs. There is never a night in the summer where the line is short and everyone happily stands on the porch waiting. They were featured on the Travel Channel and were sold recently for a few million dollars. Not bad for an ice cream store.*

5. Dishing out the chowder [PG #575]

Myrtle Beach may be mecca if you are a fan of playing golf. Take your pick of roughly 125 courses within a 25 mile radius.

With so many choices... how do you stand out in the "sea of sameness" as a local golf course?

Enter Caledonia Golf & Fish Club in Pawleys Island, South Carolina. Built in 1995, Caledonia has earned a top billing.

In Jeff Day's words:

> *"Caledonia Golf & Fish Club offers a cup of chowder at the turn, which is cooked and served right in front of you on the tenth tee – it's a unique experience. In addition, on Thursdays the course hosts a collegial public fish fry on the grounds for players to relax, eat and mingle, sharing glowing reviews of their day."*

6. Anyone for salsa? [PG #269]

This purple goldfish was submitted by Jordan Stark. Great catch:

> *"I thought of you the other day when I grabbed lunch a Moe's Southwest Grill and was pleased to find that with any of the meals you order you are given free tortilla chips and then can pick from four or five different types of salsa. This may not sound like much but over at Chipotle, the most comparable quick-food Mexican restaurant, that would cost you $2.50. Who doesn't love some free chips and salsa with their meal?"*

7. A little extra on the slide [PG #508]

This example slides in from a post by Colin Shaw of *Beyond Philosophy* {Endnote 81} :

> *Sometimes, the best ideas are the simplest ones. Inside Singapore's Changi Airport there is a four-story slide. What on earth is a slide doing in an airport? Simple – it's putting a bit of fun back into the customer experience. Spend 30 SGD within the airport, and in return you get two slide tokens. This is a great way of rewarding customers who would most likely be shopping within the airport anyway, and thus turning an automated and boring time spent waiting around, into a surprising, rewarding and entertaining experience.*
>
> *Isn't this a bit exclusive I hear you ask? What if you don't want to pay for that over-priced cup of coffee? Well, there's the smaller but free one-and-a-half story slide for the more frugal airport customers.*

8. Viva Las French Fries [#658]

Taken from a restaurant review in the Las Vegas Review Journal: {Endnote 82}

If you're even slightly tuned-in, you're no doubt aware that Michael Mina is widely regarded for his skills as a chef, most notably with fish and seafood.

But you may not know that he absolutely rocks french fries and onion rings.

No lie, french fries and onion rings, two of the standouts of our recent dinner at Stripsteak at Mandalay Bay. The skillful preparation of them proved why these two simple things — often deservedly scorned — have solid footholds in the culinary landscape.

The french fries were a lagniappe, served shortly after we ordered our wine. Fried in duck fat, they had an extreme crispness that sharpened the contrast to their fluffy interiors. They were served as a trio (a favorite Mina conceit) with one portion dusted with smoked paprika and served with barbecue sauce, one served with aioli, the other with homemade ketchup. Servers at Stripsteak point out that entrees are served a la carte, but with a lagniappe as generous as this, that point is easy to argue

9. Specially made socks keep the feet warm [PG #686]

Submitted in an e-mail by Keith Green:

"Donna just got back from Nails Plus in Little Silver (it's a chain apparently) where they give customers a free pair of socks with a purchase of a toenail painting. They are specially-made socks that go over flip flops, perfect for women getting their nails done in cold weather climates. There's a Rex Ryan joke in here somewhere…"

marketinglagniappe.com

10. A sweet hand-spun extra is on the menu [#701]

Submitted via e-mail by Matt Sheehan of *"The Good Men Project"*:

In Matt's words:

> *How are things with you? I see that the Purple Goldfish Project is moving along swimmingly (horrible joke, I know).*
>
> *Anyways, I was out to dinner in the Back Bay last week and I had a head-on collision with a piece of marketing lagniappe. Lolita, a hot new Mexican restaurant and tequila bar on Dartmouth and Boylston, gives free cotton candy with your bill at the end of the meal. They also give you a complimentary grapefruit and tequila flavored shaved ice palette cleanser when you first arrive at your table.*
>
> *The original Lolita is in Greenwich, so maybe you can take the Misses for your next date night and see what it's all about.*

11. Made from scratch and goodness [PG #700]

In the name of good eats, Jim 'n Nicks rises to the occasion from a tweet by @curbsidenick:

> *"@biteandbooze @fairelescourses @jimnnicksbbq is serious #bbq. and the unlimited cheddar corn bread is amazing. love some good #lagniappe"*

12. Benefits for both customers and prospects [PG #674]

Here is the thumbnail of the program straight from the good hands folks at Allstate: {Endnote 83}

Good Hands℠ Roadside Assistance is the first free-to-join, pay-per-use, roadside assistance service that is available to all drivers, not just Allstate customers. Allstate created Good Hands Roadside to offer protection to the 35 million American households that don't have roadside assistance services. The company also wants to provide an alternative for the 52 million households with roadside assistance that pay annual fees. Studies show the average driver uses their service only once every three years.

> *"With the launch of Good Hands Roadside, Allstate continues to broaden the definition of protection with new products and services consumers want in the ways they want them," said Chuck Paul, group vice president, Emerging Businesses, for Allstate. "This is just another option individuals can use to protect what matters most."*

Allstate suggests taking two minutes to pre-register before road "Mayhem" strikes at www.goodhandsroadside.com to improve response time.

Three Marketing Lagniappe Takeaways:

1. Build value into your lagniappe and keep it relevant. Roadside Assist is a nice compliment to the positioning of Allstate and their "good hands" promise of protection.

2. Make it easy to understand and join. The value proposition is straightforward: No fees, a reliable service and pay a low price only when you use it.

3. Benefit your customers, but open it up to prospects if possible. This is a great way to establish a relationship with future customers.

13. A free pizza and make it snappy [PG #205]

Matt Sheehan recommends the Alligator Lounge in Brooklyn. A place where the pizza is always on the house.

Here is a snippet from the *NY Magazine's* Karen Hudes on the Lounge: {Endnote 84}

> *Inside what was once the Galleria pizza place, this bar's turquoise walls, pink flamingos and Romanesque details don't quite gel, yet one crucial feature remains intact: the arched, wood-burning oven. Because of the owners' sensational idea of serving free personal pizzas every night until 3:30 a.m., this unremarkable joint has turned into a lovable hangout that's a great first or last barhop stop. Young and old Williamsburg folk congregate along the bar, in the maroon, open-angle vinyl booths, and around the green pool table. A booming jukebox and Big Buck Hunter Pro game in back provide entertainment. A selection of 10 draft beers compliments the delicious crisp-crust pies, which are on the house with every drink; toppings like pepperoni, caramelized onions and flavorful sweet sausage are available for an extra $2.*

Here is a review of the place from a customer:

> *I don't want the place to get so crowded that I can't get in. This is a fantastic place, with Widmer Hefeweizen on tap, and of course... free pizza. I didn't know about the pizza when I wandered in mid-week. When the bartender told me about it, I pictured pizza pockets... but it's wonderful wood oven thin crust pizza. You pay two bucks for your first topping and one buck for after that. I had mine loaded, so it*

set me back a whole five bucks. The same pizza in Manhattan would have set me back 15 bucks. Would I be back? I'm thinking of getting an apartment above the place!

14. Your choice of coffee or ice cream

Stew Leonard's is a grocery store without peer. It personifies the concept of marketing lagniappe. There are a handful of extras the store offers, but my favorite is the free ice cream or coffee with a purchase of $100 or more in groceries. It's that little extra or "WOW" according to Stew that makes all the difference.

I had the opportunity to hear Stew recount a great story about the power of word of mouth:

> *About 40 years ago Stew was asked by the local elementary school to come out and speak on Career Day. The principal asked him to talk about the milk business. As Stew pulled into the parking lot he saw a fire truck parked in front of the school with kids all around it. When he walked through the door he saw a room about the Air Force playing a movie with jet airplanes. It was filled with kids. Across the hall was a police officer and he was showing a packed classroom about various police equipment and weapons. Soon he walked down the hall and found his classroom with a sign on the door that read "THE MILK BUSINESS". Stew walked in the room to find only three kids sitting there, two of which were the sons of one of his managers. For the next 30 minutes he talked about the dairy business and running a store. At the end of the talk he thanked the kids, reaching into his pocket and handing them each a coupon for a free ice cream. The kids left and Stew waited in his classroom for the second of the two Career Day sessions. He waited and waited... no kids. After a while the principal came rushing in, "Stew... I don't know what you told those kids, but we have to move your next session to the school auditorium."*

15. A very nice school of flying purple goldfish [PG #579]

JetBlue builds value into their flight offerings. They know the little things can make the biggest impact. They understand it takes more than the proverbial half can of soda.

Let's look at each "differentiator":

- *Full can of soda and unlimited brand name snacks.* What's with the cup of ice with some soda in it by other airlines? You wouldn't put up with that treatment on the ground.
- *First bag free.* Southwest has done an amazing job of promoting that "Bags Fly Free", but JetBlue is singing from the same prayer sheet. Saving customers either $25 or $50 per round trip is an added value.
- *36 channels* that allow you to watch... when you want to watch them. JetBlue gives you the two things that traditional air travel takes away: CHOICE and CONTROL.
- *The most legroom in coach.* Being 6'2" I can tell you this is key. Nothing more annoying than the person in front of you reclining into your kneecaps.
- Direct flights. Avoiding layovers is key. It saves time, hassle and annoyance.

16. Pioneers in handshake marketing [PG #295]

I came across Umpqua Bank in Joseph Jaffe's book *Flip the Funnel.* {Endnote 85} Umpqua understands branded acts of kindness and takes the concept "to the bank."

The chain based in Portland, Oregon has tellers place customers' cash on black wooden trays along with a silver chocolate coin embellished with the bank's logo. Add in free wifi, plus their own brand of free gourmet coffee and you've got some very purple goldfish.

17. One more flying Goldfish for good measure [PG #773]

Submitted via e-mail by Gene Willis:

> *"KLM gives Delft Blue Houses to customers who fly business class."*

Here is a little additional background on the history of the houses courtesy of Theo Kiewiet: {Endnote 86}

> *The KLM houses are presents to travelers aboard KLM flights in Business and Royal Class. They have been presented over a long period and thus have become collector items. There are currently over 90 different types which are each individually numbered in order of release.*
>
> *There is Dutch Genever, 35% alcohol, in the houses, which are in fact bottles with a cork and seal on top. Sometimes the genever has been drunk but mostly the empty bottles were empty all along. On flights to some countries with strict alcohol restrictions empty houses are presented. On some of the houses a sticker explains this by referring to customs regulations. Sometimes there is a cork and seal and sometimes there isn't (and never was) on the empty bottles.*
>
> *KLM started issuing these miniature bottles in 1952. Airlines were not allowed to give presents to their customers because of unfair competition. So, KLM had some Blue Delft*

houses made, and filled them with genever (gin). Then, of course, their competitors complained, "KLM is giving presents to their customers." KLM said, "May we decide how we serve our drinks? Is their a law which tells me drinks have to be served in a glass?"… and so it all started.

Chapter 14

#2 - Thinking Outside the Bowl

"Here is a simple but powerful rule: always give people more than what they expect to get."
- Nelson Boswel

The second type of purple goldfish involves those **In the Bag / Out of the Box**. These are little unexpected things that are given as a surprise.

Let's look at eight examples:

1. It's all in the design and details [PG #636]

Spotlight: Johnny Cupcakes bakes its way via a tweet by David Knies @davidknies:

> *"@9INCHmarketing stan check out @johnnycupcakes and what they do in their shipments to customers!"*

It turns out that Johnny Cupcakes spends time creating a few purple goldfish to accompany his mail order shipments. Here is a comment from a forum: {Endnote 86}

> *"What a great display. So, there was a. the box, b. the tissue paper, c. the bag, d. the shirt, e. the hang tag, f. the oven mitt label, g. the home alone card, h. the business card, i. the button, and j. the candy."*

Wait a second... I didn't see any cupcakes in that package??? Turns out that Cupcakes is Johnny's nickname. His name is Earle and Johnny Earle doesn't make cupcakes. He makes T-shirts and Johnny knows marketing.

Here are three marketing takeaways from Johnny Cupcakes:

> 1. **Details, details, details** – Johnny understands that you need to do the little things to stand out in a sea of sameness.

You need to create an experience for your customers and make your brand talkable. The product in ovens + bakery counters, the oven mitt hang tags, the takeout boxes and the 80's T-shirt designs all play a part in creating the Johnny Cupcakes brand.

2. **Keep it fresh and limited** – Despite numerous offers by department and specialty stores, Johnny prefers to keep it personal and only sells his products online or in his four stores (hometown of Hull, Boston, Los Angeles and London). All of his shirts are limited editions, some of which are runs of 100 or less.

3. **Be approachable and take care of your fans** – Part of Johnny's appeal is his personal story of a scrappy kid selling T-shirts out of an '86 Toyota. He's an American success story of following your passion. Johnny makes himself accessible by blogging, releasing videos and even hosting customer appreciation events.

2. Minty Fresh and Packed with Detail [PG #437]

Courtesy of University of North Carolina Professor Joe Bob Hester @joebobhester. Joe Bob forwarded this article from Ron Green Jr. at the Charlotte Observer. {Endnote 87} It highlights the apparel brand Peter Millar and its founder Scott Knott.

Here is an excerpt:

> **"They remember the mints."**
>
> *When boxes of golf shirts and shorts and other high-end menswear are shipped from the Peter Millar office and warehouse, the packing list includes mints.*
>
> *When customers unpack their orders, they are struck by three things: The quality of what they've ordered; each item comes out of the box in the order it's listed on the packing sheet; and, mints are included for the pleasure of it.*

It's a little thing but this year when a few boxes arrived short of mints (they ran out briefly), phone calls started coming.

At Peter Millar, located in a low-profile office park on the southwest edge of Raleigh, the attention to detail, commitment to quality and a North Carolina-grown appreciation of classic menswear has helped catapult the company into one of the hottest brands on the market, particularly for golfers.

3. Adopt a Finger Puppet [PG #549]

In the words of Ariel Savrin-Jacobs:

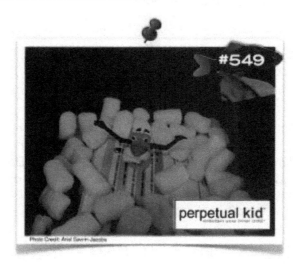

I spoke to you after blogging about your purple goldfish project {Endnote 88} this summer when I interned for STELLAService. I'm happy to finally say I've found a purple goldfish! I checked your list, so if it's updated I think this is a new one.

Last week I bought a few fun things online for my dorm room from PerpetualKid.com. It was my first time buying from them, and I'll certainly be a repeat customer. The site is overall really fun (for example, I got measuring cups that stack like a Russian nesting doll), and it definitely didn't hurt that my order placed at 10:00 p.m. on the 18th, shipped the next morning and arrived on the 20th. But the best part of it all was the surprise "finger monster" (for lack of better words) sitting on top when I opened the package. While I don't quite know what to do with it, I sure got a kick out of it, and I bet many other customers probably did too. I've attached a picture of this rubber "finger monster." Hope it helps on your way to 1,001 and I will let you know if I come across any others!

4. A saucy purple goldfish [PG #223]

A fixed tasting menu, legendary meatballs, free wine and a jar of sauce makes Maroni Cuisine a Long Island Legend. Maroni Cuisine of Northport pours into the Purple Goldfish Project courtesy of Clark Johnson:

Maroni Cuisine in Northport, NY is consistently rated by Zagat voters as either the best or among the best restaurants on Long Island. Mike Maroni beat Bobby Flay in a throwdown! The meals are exclusively customized tasting menus, prix fixe, with all the wine you can drink included. At the end of the meal, hours later, guests are generally presented with jars of Maroni Pasta sauce as a "Thank You." Once you have used it, you want to go back for more (both the meal and the sauce!)

5. This Goldfish Has Balls (three of them to be exact) [PG #245]

Will Prest is from Minneapolis and he shared this gem from the Twin Cities.

Michael Lynne's Tennis Shop

"When you pick up your professionally strung racquet, you get a new can of Penn balls with the Michael Lynne Tennis

logo and name in big letters on it. It is a nice gesture, plus his balls are left all over the clubs around town. Here is the website. {Endnote 89} It got me to visit the site and I read a few of the articles on there… they were a nice surprise."

Companies that tend to really get the concept of marketing lagniappe, tend to have multiple examples in their arsenal. Maybe it has something to do with fish wanting to swim in schools.

Here is an excerpt from an article about Michael Lynne in a tennis industry publication:

It's not only about sales. Fully supportive of Minneapolis' large tennis community, Lynne puts kids' and local team photos on his back wall along with local tennis stories and news. And he's happy to offer tennis tips to his customers and encourages them to "test drive" racquets for free.

Clothing is grouped by size and the price is always visible. Racks are never overcrowded and pieces are displayed on the wall so customers can see them as "outfits." When customers try on clothes, they find large dressing rooms with excellent lighting. Also, all the employees don various tennis outfits to work so customers can see what the clothes actually look like "on."

The store also has six stringing machines, so, as Michael notes, "You can have your racquets strung while you wait." But even "waiting" at Michael Lynne's Tennis Shop is a pleasure. Customers can watch the Tennis Channel on TV while having a snack or sipping gourmet coffee the shop supplies.

"We're a destination point," Lynne says. "People have to drive here, so we want to make sure our staff is well-informed on the merchandise and offers great customer service."

"Michael and Mimzy personify customer service, and they teach their staff to take this approach," says Greg Mason, senior director of sales for HEAD. "It's the little things like greeting each customer, then thanking them as they leave,

writing thank-you notes to repeat customers — that really makes the difference."

The staff is always upbeat and motivated. "It's apparent they get it," says Mason. "The Minneapolis tennis market is the real winner."

Let me count the *purple goldfish*:

1. Free balls with restringing
2. Free racquet demo's
3. Stringing while you wait in style
4. Large well lit dressing rooms
5. Handwritten thank you notes.

I love the second to last paragraph of the article, "It's the little things... that make the biggest difference." **AMEN**

6. A welcome little extra with your sugar and spice [PG #718]

Taken from a tweet about Penzey's Spices by @nelderini

"Bumpersticker lagniappe included in my peppercorns order from Penzey's. Classy. Love those guys."

7. Call me… [PG #988]

Submitted via e-mail by Vanessa Khedouri:

> *Rebecca Minkoff bags all have an extra business card in them – it has a guy's picture and on the back there is a handwritten note that says "call me", signed by "Vincent" with a phone number When you call [give it a try at +1 646 420 1475], there is a recording of a message from "Vincent" – a guy with a sexy French accent – who references his friend, "Rebecca" (the designer) and her website. I love that touch and it feels personal!*

According to Rebecca Minkoff:

> *"I find cute pics and have them printed on cards and people actually do call! When customers call they hear a guy's voice and he is French. Some people call and think they met the guy the night before. It's kind of funny to hear some of the messages!"*

8. The little extra here is in the bag [PG #772]

Submitted via e-mail by Will Villota:

> *"Haven't heard it called lagniappe, but Zipcar sometimes leaves gift bags in random cars. Customers reporting that they found them also receive bonus Zipcar time. Hope this helps!"*

Chapter 15

#3 - Sampling

"One of the best ways to motivate consumers to try new products is through sampling. Once a consumer tries a new product through sampling, it's likely they will add it to their shopping list."

- Julie Hall

Sampling is the lowest hanging fruit in marketing

There may not be a more cost effective way for brands to drive purchase intent and conversion than sampling.

The proof is in the numbers as highlighted in this article in *BRANDWEEK* {Endnote 90}. Here are the top two takeaways from the Arbitron survey:

- 24% of consumers bought the product they sampled instead of the item they initially set out to purchase.
- 35% of customers who tried a sample bought the product during the same shopping trip.

But why does sampling just have to be about the prospect? Why can't you leverage current customers with an additional little extra to increase satisfaction, drive retention and promote word of mouth?

Let's look at a seven companies who do exactly that:

1. This purple goldfish has a fragrant bouquet [PG #505]

Submitted by Frances Lewis: **Sephora**

> Thanks so much for the MENG webinar. {Endnote 91} Laughed out loud — I had "three or more" moments in the last week — stayed at a DoubleTree (though had great experience with housekeeping as well as a cookie) and ate at Five Guys.

103

My third was Sephora — was searching for a perfume for a gift, and salesperson not only gave great "traditional" assistance, but created customized samples in little spray containers, then bagged and labeled them.

I grew up in New Orleans and remember "lagniappe" very often as a tray of hard candies given in lieu of a penny's change. Great concept.

The act of creating customized samples is a nice touch on behalf of Sephora. If Sephora leverages it in cosmetics... then Kiehl's absolutely wields it to great effect. **[PG #528]** According to *Real Simple* magazine, {Endnote 92}

> *"Kiehl's hands out samples of every product it sells — approximately 10 million giveaways a year."*

Kiehl's samples in four different ways:

1. At a Kiehl's store.
2. At a Kiehl's counter in a department store.
3. Over the phone
4. Online

What was the third one again? Call Kiehl's and tell the operator what you'd like to try and the company will send you up to three samples. If you don't believe it, here's the number +1 800 543 4572.

According to Kiehl's website:

We understand that no two skin or hair types are exactly alike and that products work differently for each person. To ensure you find the precise products that meet your needs, Kiehl's pioneered an extensive Sampling Program many years ago. We're confident that when you try our products, you will recognize the high quality and efficacy of the preparation. We invite you to try three Kiehl's samples with your first order of the day to discover other Kiehl's formulations from our extensive line of skin, hair and body care.

2. This one brings a little extra flavor [#582]

Submitted by Katie Morrow of Aveus: **Izzy's**

> *"Izzy's ice cream shop in St. Paul, Minnesota offers a free 'Izzy' with each scoop order. Every scoop gets a free 'Izzy' – a mini scoop of another flavor on top."*

Izzy's Ice Cream is an iconic ice cream store in St. Paul. The owner Jeff Sommers was told to do two things when he opened his shop:

1. Smile... and
2. Give away samples

Jeff disliked the idea of just giving away free samples, so he created his own wrinkle. Customers are allowed to add an IZZY scoop with each scoop purchased. It's a small scoop of any flavor. Great for customers who can take a "worry free" chance to try a new flavor. It's a little extra that goes a long way. Don't take my word for it, Izzy's was voted the best ice cream shop in America by *Reader's Digest.*

3. Tee Time [PG #378]

Bigelow Tea was submitted by Jack Campisi,

> *I found a Purple Goldfish in a box of tea today. I opened a new box of Bigelow Vanilla Chai Tea and I was surprised to see a different colored label on the tea bag I pulled out. I wondered if I had bought the wrong flavor, but it turns out it was a bonus bag of their "Constant Comment" Orange Spiced Chai Tea.*

> *It was a nice surprise and a great chance for me to sample another variety of their tea without having to buy an box of a flavor I may not like. And the good news is that I liked it.*

> *This is a great example of lagniappe because it surprised and delighted me and it was very relevant. If they had not done that, I probably never would have tried that kind of tea... but now I*

just might go get a box. *So mission accomplished Bigelow; you made a customer happy, turned me on to another one of your products and you are generating word of mouth buzz. That's a Purple Goldfish.*

4. Try something new . . . on the house [PG #512]

Courtesy of my neighbor Eric Wiberg: **Nagoya Restaurant**

Every time Nagoya Japanese restaurant in SoNo [South Norwalk, CT] delivers their (excellent) food, they add a "compliments of the house" special freebie, which is always high quality, always different and always elicits gratitude. The freebie ranges from complex California sushi roll type samples to edamame, a dessert, or a soup. They are small but of high quality.

The freebies introduce us to foods we would not normally try and always make us eager to open the delivery and see what is in store for us. On each gift is a simple black magic marker saying "on the house" or "house special". They have never mentioned it on the phone or delivery person, never failed to include it, and never asked for anything in return.

In return we give them our total loyalty for all Asian food purchases for our house and guests. We've never even eaten in the restaurant or met the staff (aside from friendly drivers) but because of this simple "Purple Goldfish" gesture, we are die-hard fans of Nagoya of SoNo and suspect that we are not the only recipients of their discreet kindness.

5. A Guarantee, Free Gift Wrapping, Handwritten Notes and all the Nonpareils You Can Eat In-Store [PG #225]

Cheryl Ahto offers up Josh Early Candies. A *sweet* example of marketing lagniappe:

Word of mouth marketing will get you into the store. Sampling their famous nonpareils will turn you into a repeat

106

customer before you've even walked out the door. Josh Early Candies is a fifth generation family business based in Allentown, Pennsylvania and they understand marketing lagniappe. The quality of their candy and their friendly, hard-working sales people make for an unforgettable customer experience. But it's the purple goldfish – the free, incredibly delicious, nonpareils that will keep you coming back for more. Believe me. I've been buying their chocolate for decades!

Fantastic example. Josh Early Candies is a Lehigh Valley institution. Cheryl sent me a box of the nonpareils as a "thank you." There a few things in life that can live up to high expectations... Josh Early nonpareils needs to be added to the list. Hand-made chocolates with hand-made extras.

6. Smell, see it, touch it and taste it [PG #383]

In the words of Nicolas Nelson:

The Great Harvest Bakery is a relatively small franchise chain of wonderful American-style bakeries that is growing slowly on purpose–they want to make extra sure that every new Great Harvest Bakery is top notch and fully reflects the ethos of the original one.

Lagniappe is what Great Harvest Bakery is all about– it comes across in a dozen ways. But the first one any visitor will notice immediately is the free bread tasting every time you come in the door. Yep, everyone who even stops by gets a free slice of their choice of the day's fresh-baked bread. A generous free slice.

Whether or not you buy something. Whether or not you even stay in the bakery after you take their bread. Whether or not you say thank you. Free bread, every visit! Of course, there's a catch: the bread is unbelievably good. That free slice of bread will convince you to buy a whole loaf. We do, almost every week. The panini sandwiches are pretty amazing too, by the way (but not free).

Marketing Lagniappe Takeaway: As a general rule, "People don't know what they like... they like what they know." You need to figure ways to get people to try new products. Make it easy and risk free. Great Harvest gets to pick the bread of the day and let customers experience something new.

7. Try a new coffee or tea drink while in line [PG #351]

#351 in the Project is submitted by Ted Simon:

Starbucks in Terra Linda

> *"When the line gets really long, it's common for one of the staff to come out with a tray of complimentary samples of the latest and greatest beverage. A nice treat while you wait."*

Chapter 16

#4 - First / Last Impressions

*"We don't know where our first impressions
come from or precisely what they mean,
so we don't always appreciate their fragility."*

- Malcolm Gladwell

THE POWER OF PRIMACY AND RECENCY

One of the foundations of marketing lagniappe is the idea of leveraging primacy and recency. They say (*whoever they are*) that people tend to remember the first thing and the last thing they see. A ton of attention is paid to the importance of a first impression (primacy), but little is made of the last moment (recency). The concept of doing a little unexpected extra at the time of purchase is a recency strategy. This is partly explained by Nobel Prize Winner Danial Kahneman as the Peak-End Rule. {Endnote 93} Kahneman believes that we judge our past experiences almost entirely on how they were at their peak (whether pleasant or unpleasant) and how they ended.

According to Forbes columnist Dean Crutchfield, {Endnote 94}

> *"Designing for the peak-end rule is another way of not focusing on what is less important, but about focusing on what brings the most value to the customer experience. In other words, make sure that your peak and end is memorable, branded and differentiated."*

You never get a second chance to make a first or last impression. ***Translation:*** You need give the customer something to talk, tweet, blog, Yelp or Facebook about right before they leave, hang up or log out.

Let's look at six examples:

1. How does a hotel launch itself all the way to #6 on the *Conde Nast* Readers Choice Best List? [PG #185]

Answer: Lots of Amazing Glass and Service that's First Class

Mark Brooks wrote an excellent post about the Hotel Murano on LostRemote.com. {Endnote 95} Here is an excerpt:

> *A friend of mine, Brian Forth, recently made a reservation at the Hotel Murano in Tacoma, Washington... After making the reservation, Brian tweeted about how he was looking forward to having a stay-cation with his wife in honor of his birthday. When the couple entered the hotel, they were greeted by name and given an automatic upgrade at no charge. When they entered the room, they found a welcome package including gourmet cupcakes. Naturally, Brian tweeted some more about all the nice surprises.*
>
> *Upon check-in, he inquired about whether the hotel shuttle would ferry he and his wife to a local steakhouse for dinner. Later, he posted the same question on Twitter. About three minutes afterward, the phone rang in his room and the concierge informed him that the shuttle would be available whenever it was needed.*
>
> *So Brian tweeted again. And the culmination of those tweets, from [Brian] a respected local business owner, had arguably more marketing power than any local advertisement the hotel could have purchased with the money they spent making Brian and his wife happy. Think about it: the cupcakes cost $5, the rest of it was just awareness and hustle.*

Give them something to talk, tweet, post and Facebook about

Mark talked about how the Hotel Murano was voted #6 on the *Condé Nast Traveler's* Reader's Choice list. {Endnote 96} He went on further to state that this distinction has puzzled many of the locals, especially those in Seattle. So – how do they do it?

The proof is in the pudding... or maybe in the cupcakes. The companies who understand marketing lagniappe tend to get the little things right. Whether it's greeting a first time customer by name (they probably had Brian's picture from his Twitter address @brainfroth), to a complimentary room upgrade or a shuttle ride... the Hotel Murano gets it.

By the way – in case you feel you might be missing out on those miles or points [a.k.a Ryan Bingham syndrome, {Endnote 97}] just whip out another hotel loyalty card and the Hotel Murano will hook you up with some immediate swag.

2. Going Above and Beyond to Get it Right [PG #141]

Submitted by Mark True:

> *"On the two occasions I stayed there, The Hotel Burnham in downtown Chicago left me a bottle of wine and then a bottle of root beer with a personal note from the manager. The root beer was the second gift, after I thanked them for the wine and told them that I'm not a wine drinker after the first visit!"*

[Nice personal touch by the Hotel Burnham... kudos for getting it right the second time around as a great lagniappe isn't a "one size fits all proposition"]

3. What's Your Cold Drink? [PG #605]

Taken from a blog post by Business Voice: {Endnote 98}

> One of our many great clients is Mountain View Tire, a 29-store tire and automotive service company in southern California. The other day I was adding testimonials to the new website we just built for them when I saw this one:
>
> > *"I wanted to make it known that I received exceptional service beyond anything I could have ever expected from your [store] in Burbank, California.*

111

I was heading to Lebec, California and blew out my tire just north of Burbank. I called the Magnolia [Road] location and spoke with Leville Slayton. He dispatched Jacob Pomaville to my location where he retrieved the tire from my vehicle, brought it back to the store, replaced the tire, and repaired the wheel.

Amid this stressful situation, Jacob had a cold drink ready for me and, beyond that, actually purchased two jack stands from a nearby auto parts store, as neither one of us had them.

I wanted to share this story with you as it is a rarity, especially in the Los Angeles area. They have secured me as a new customer with their exceptional service and care."

I know the folks at Mountain View Tire pride themselves on providing "the WOW experience" for their customers, but the fact that Jacob brought the stranded customer a cold drink just blew me away!

It shows that he was thoughtful enough to anticipate what the customer may have needed, given what he was experiencing: the flat tire, the hot sun, being stranded, the feelings of frustration! (You've probably been there. So think how you'd feel if Jacob showed up, not only to fix your tire, but with free refreshments!) The customer needed relief, both physically and emotionally, and Jacob was intuitive enough – or trained well enough – to understand and react to those needs.

Nothing calculated. Nothing out of the Mountain View marketing plan. Just a 99-cent bottle of water or pop that secured me as a new customer. Perfect.

What about your company? How are you delivering "cold drinks" to your customers? Again, it's not something that has to be "part of the plan," but, for it to work on a sincere, memorable human level, the question "how can I best serve my customer today" needs to be part of your company's DNA. When that question permeates your culture and your staff works every day to answer it, you'll garner the type of loyalty and earn the good word of mouth that Mountain View Tire does.

4. Surprise "thank you"... your bill is half off [PG #355]

Submitted via e-mail by Owen Clark:

In Owen's words:

> *In Roseville, CA, Arigato offers half-priced sushi, all the time. Started as a promotion when the place opened but business was so successful they never got rid of it. Even though I know it's permanent it still makes you feel like your getting a great value every time you go in.*
>
> *Especially because the menu still has the full-prices and you don't really see the savings until you get the bill. Also, sushi is good enough that they could be charging a lot more.*

Marketing Lagniappe Takeaway: Half off every day is a distinctive pricing model. It looks like a "wink, wink" in the know play. You only see the discount when your bill is presented. Talk about surprise and delight for a first timer.

5. Move over plain old mint . . . [PG #762]

Taken from a post by Lou Imbriano {Endnote 99} about the Hard Rock Hotel at Universal Studios Orlando:

> *"Another fun amenity of staying at the Hard Rock Hotel at Universal is that instead of finding mints left on your pillow each night before bed, you discover guitar picks, funky bracelets, or smiley faced super balls, giving a new meaning to "have a nice day."*

6. SPICY MAC, A TINFOIL SWAN & OYSTER SHOOOOOTERS! [PG #226]

Tucked under the Morrison Bridge in Portland is a restaurant that boasts a handful of purple goldfish.

Here are three of my favorites from Le Bistro Montage:

1. A signature dish in Spam and Mac. Macaroni & Cheese with your favorite mystery canned meat. For a little lagniappe on the flavor... you can order it SPICY.

2. Oyster and Mussel Shooters – slimy fellas served in a shot glass with some cocktail sauce and horseradish. Once ordered – the waiter or waitress will immediately scream to the kitchen... OYSTER SHOOOOOTER.

3. Your leftovers get wrapped up in tin foil. Move over balloon animal guy, the staff at the Bistro will "WOW" you with their animals.

Chapter 17

#5 - Guarantees

*"Truth is that you don't know what is going to happen tomorrow.
Life is a crazy ride, and nothing is guaranteed."*

- Eminem

STANDING BEHIND YOUR PRODUCT OR SERVICE

The fifth type of Purple Goldfish involves "Guarantees." The little extra commitment that you will stand behind your product or service.

Let's look at a few examples:

1. Lifetime Commitment [PG #800]

Leon Leonwood Bean was an avid hunter and fisherman in Freeport, Maine. During his outdoor activities he noticed that his boots would become soaked. In 1911, the 39 year old Bean set out to solve this problem and developed plans for a waterproof boot. The Bean boot was a combination of lightweight leather for the upper part of the boot and rubber on the bottom. He brought the plans to a cobbler and the first boots were made. Bean felt the boot produced to be of good quality, obtained a list of non-resident Maine hunting license holders and prepared a descriptive mail order circular (His first catalogue was a whopping 4 pages). He promised 100% money back for anyone who was unhappy with the boots. Because of this, Bean had to *refund 90% of the first 100 sets of boots* made, when the rubber on the bottom developed cracks. Bean seemed not to mind returning the money, the popularity of the boots was clear.

Barry Dalton relays a wonderful story about L.L. Bean:

> *My friends recently decided to take up hiking the Appalachian Trail as a hobby. I could probably think of about 3 dozen more leisurely activities to pick up as a "hobby". But awesome for them!*
>
> *So, about sixty or seventy miles into their latest trek last week, they were strolling within a few miles of my house and asked to camp for the night for a hot meal and a shower. So, after devouring half the food in the house and getting cleaned up, we all sat down with a bottle of wine to hear some stories.*
>
> *My friend proceeds to tell me that at a campground, he and a fellow hiker got their Bean Boot laces crossed, whereby the stranger ended up accidentally putting my friends boots into his backpack and hauling off down the trail. My friend, upon later putting his fellow long-departed sojourner's size 14 boots on his size nine foot realized the mix up.*
>
> *He called L.L. Bean from the trail (in our connected world were no place is "out of range") and told them of his dilemma. The Bean rep told him that he would FedEx a new pair of boots in the right size to my address for next day*

delivery. In return, they asked him to send the old boots back to them when he got back home.

Oh, did I mention that they treated this like an exchange? Like… he didn't have to buy the new pair of boots. And get this: The boots they were sending him cost 30 bucks less than the old ratty size 14's he had in his sack. So, Bean sent him a gift card for the 30 bucks! I couldn't make this stuff up!

We finish the wine (and one or two more bottles, I think), went to sleep. And sure enough, around 10:00 a.m. the next day, the FedEx guy delivered a brand new pair of warm, dry Bean Boots to my door.

So, do you think my friend will buy his next 10 pair of boots, and all his other outdoor, Daniel Boone, trail-blazing gear from L.L. Bean for the rest of his hiking days?

Sometimes 'NO' isn't a bad thing. In fact when it comes to free shipping and guarantees, how about **no** minimum orders for free shipping and **no** end date on guarantees. Throw in 'no conditions' for lagniappe. Kudos to L.L. Bean.

2. Replace or repair and have fun [PG #835]

JanSport via a tweet by @markosul:

"Just received a notice from JanSport "thanking us" for returning a "vintage" backpack; they are sending us a new 1 free"

It's more than a bag. It's a JanSport. A guarantee that carries on for the life of the backpack.

Here's a story from a post by the alaskanlibrarian: {Endnote 100}

"Recently the JanSport backpack I've used for a number of years suffered "zipper disease" where it simply wouldn't stay zipped. I went to the JanSport web site and looked up their lifetime warranty information. It took me a week or so to box

up and mail my backpack. JanSport sent me a postcard when they received my backpack. Last Friday, about a week after the postcard, my backpack arrived in the mail. JanSport replaced my zipper free of charge and shipped it free to Alaska! It works as good as new. If you need a backpack, buy JanSport. It's a great product backed by great service. And yes, I've bought more than one backpack from them."

Another great customer story. The account by Hillary Lipko at The Frustrated Bunny {Endnote 101} shows how JanSport goes above and beyond:

I got my backpack back from JanSport yesterday, and I must say that I am more than impressed with the quality of the repairs. In fact, I'd say that they went well above and beyond the repairs I sent it in for. In the letter that I included with the backpack when I sent it, the only repairs I mentioned were that it needed the main compartment zipper replaced, and I needed the straps replaced. The zipper had contracted the dreaded "zipper disease," and the foam in the straps had compressed so much that it might as well not have been there anymore. (Provided, these problems had occurred after about eight years of continuous use, which I think is pretty damn good.) Not only did they fix these things well beyond my satisfaction, they also replaced the handle on the top of the bag, the zipper pull that had broken off the front pocket, and the fraying of the fabric on some of the inside seams of the bag. None of those things bothered me, but I am beyond pleased that their repair center apparently takes time to assess the returned bag for everything that needs fixing rather than just relying on what the customer tells them.

Marketing Lagniappe Takeaways: Stand behind your product for life. Fix mistakes or issues while keeping the customer informed. Look for ways to deliver above and beyond to exceed expectations. Have fun in the process.

3. Guarantees designed to make you a customer for life [PG #460]

Jeanne Bliss offered up Zane's during a speech at a Net Promoter conference {Endnote 102}.

Free tune ups and lifetime warranty. Here's the breakdown from founder Chris Zane:

> *"Every bicycle purchased from Zane's Cycles comes with our exclusive Lifetime Free Service and Lifetime Parts Warranty. Anytime your bicycle needs service, a full tune-up or just a quick adjustment, we will make those necessary adjustments for free as long as you own your bicycle."*

The guarantee doesn't just stop there. Zane's also offers:

- *90-Day Price Protection. We guarantee you will never overpay at Zane's Cycles. If you find any item you purchased in stock for less anywhere in Connecticut within 90 days, we'll gladly refund you the difference, plus an additional 10% in cash.*

- *30 Day Test Ride. To guarantee you have purchased the correct bicycle, ride it for 30 days. If during that time you are not completely satisfied, please return the bicycle for an exchange. We will gladly give you a full credit toward your new selection.*

- *Serious. Fun. Guaranteed. Twenty five + years ago we started with the belief, "the only difference between us and our competition is the service that we offer." If you don't feel that we are living up to our mission, let us know and we'll fix it immediately. If you have a concern and would like to discuss it with me directly, please e-mail me. I will personally respond to you.*

Chapter 18

#6 - Pay it Forward

"One of the deep secrets of life is that all that is really worth doing is what we do for others."

- Lewis Carroll

GIVING BACK AND PAYING IT FORWARD

Sometimes the little extra is not about the customer, but rather giving back to the community or to those in need.

Let's look at a handful of examples:

1. Right from the Heart [PG #123]

Plaza Cleaners in Portland, Oregon submitted by Blue Young:

"I think it counts, though it's not so typical. They will clean someone's suit for free if they're unemployed and need the suit for a job interview."

2. ONE BAG, ONE BOOK [PG #432]

Tyson Adams helps people with a simple premise. His company liveGLOCAL lands in the Purple Goldfish Project with a feel good extra.

"With every bag of coffee you purchase, liveGLOCAL gives one book to a child in need."

3. Honoring the Troops [PG #782]

Coffee Bean & Tea Leaf was submitted via e-mail by Ryan Macaulay of Epic Sports. In Ryan's words:

"At Coffee Bean & Tea Leaf in LA, if you buy a bag of coffee to support our troops overseas, {Endnote 103} Coffee Bean will buy your round of coffees at the time of purchase. Even better, there is a blank white area on the actual coffee bag designated specifically for you to write a personal message to the troops the coffee is going to!"

4. Save $$$ and plant up to a dozen trees a year... Chegg gets top grades [PG #235]

Chegg chuggs into the Purple Goldfish Project from the folks over at Gaspedal: {Endnote 104}

College students love Chegg for their cheap textbook rentals, free shipping, and eco-friendly business philosophy. Chegg believes that renting a book instead of buying it new helps save trees. This isn't just their corporate mission statement, the company actually functions around this core value. For every book they rent, they plant a tree in return. As the customer finishes their transaction, Chegg presents a world map and asks the customer to pick a country or region to plant their tree in. It's a simple, visual way of engaging during the transaction process and giving back to the community at the same time. Customers can then tell the world what they did by linking their Chegg transaction to their Facebook *profile or Twitter account.*

5. Give to Get [PG #149]

If you gave a day of volunteer service to a participating organization in 2010, you received one day of free admission to a Disney Park. The folks at Disney called this first-of-its-kind program, "Give a Day, Get a Disney Day." {Endnote 105}

The premise is simple and straightforward - a free one-day ticket to a Disneyland or Walt Disney World theme park for guests who volunteer a day of service to a participating organization.

Chapter 19

#7 - Thank You / Follow Up

"Learn to say thank you every time."

-Jill Griffi

FOLLOWING UP AND SAYING "THANK YOU"

After covering six "value" PG's, this chapter marks the first type of *"maintenance"* focused Purple Goldfish. The seventh Purple Goldfish is the expression of thanks to a customer. A personal gesture that conveys both appreciation and acknowledgement.

Let's look at 9 examples:

1. The power of the pen... and some stickers [PG #770]

Gary Vaynerchuk's offers up Wufoo in his book, *The Thank You Economy*. {Endnote 106} The online HTML form developer sends handwritten thank you notes, sometimes crafted out of construction paper and decorated with stickers.

2. A simple way to "Hug Your Customers" [PG #805]

Taken from a tweet by Annette Franz @annettefranz

Annette cites *1to1* media's post on Mitchells by Ginger Conlon: {Endnote 107}

> *When was the last time you personally thanked a customer? Sent a handwritten note? Last year Jack Mitchell wrote 1,793 personal notes to customers of his retail stores. That's about five notes a day, every day.*

Mitchell is CEO of The Mitchells Family of Stores, which owns several high-end retail stores, including Marsh, Mitchells, and Richards–and is author of Hug Your Customers. He spoke at the Conference Board Customer Experience Leadership Conference about connecting with customers on a more personal level.

Every touch-point, every interaction, every detail–these are all opportunities to connect with customers in way that creates engagement and builds retention. "It can be something as simple as a smile," Mitchell said. "It's about making a human connection. Connections are 'hugs.' And hugs create loyalty."

So do great people, he said. Great product is a given; personalized service is where you can really make a difference. So the company looks for people who are honest, positive, competent, and nice, and have a passion to listen, learn, and grow. The retailer retains and engages it employees by using them in catalogs and ads, and by providing them with the product and customer information they need to deliver outstanding service. Also, there's no commission, which encourages collaboration. "It [all] helps to increase their commitment to customer service," he said.

A technology backbone is the third leg of the customer experience stool. The company has tracked every purchase by SKU since 1989, and as a result, has a comprehensive database of customers' product and channel preferences– and knows exactly who its top customers are, by spend. The company uses the information to create personalized mailings, send relevant event invitations (e.g., trunk shows), and the like.

This blended high-touch, high-tech approach helps keep customers right where Mitchell wants them–at center of the company's universe–because customer centricity, he said, is profitable. In fact, 72 percent of the retailer's merchandise is sold at full price. "Focus on what's most important," he said. "Customers."

126

3. Save the date stickers are an added touch [PG #332]

From a subscriber of the Metropolis Performing Arts Center:

> *"We have season tickets to our local theater, Metropolis Performing Arts in Arlington Heights, IL. When we receive the tickets in the mail, included are round Metropolis stickers that I can use to put on my calendar to remember our theater nights."*

4. A little thoughtful personal touch from the Captain [PG #710]

Taken from a blog post by Ivan Misner: {Endnote 108}

> Long lines, deteriorating service, flight attendants grabbing a beer and pulling the emergency exit handle to slide out onto the tarmac are part of our vision of airlines these days.
>
> However, I had an experience last week that was truly amazing in this day and age. My wife and I were flying on United from LAX to New Orleans for a business conference. Before we were about to land, Rebecca, the flight attendant, handed me a business card from the Captain. His name is Patrick Fletcher. On the back of Captain Fletcher's card was a handwritten note that said:
>
> > *Flight 139, January 19, 2011*
> >
> > *Mr. and Mrs. Misner,*
> >
> > *It's great to have you both with us today – Welcome! I hope you have a great visit to New Orleans – we really appreciate your business!*
> >
> > *Sincerely,*
> >
> > *Pat Fletcher*

Rebecca (who was a great flight attendant, by the way), told me the Captain wrote these notes to everyone who was a member of their premier level frequent flier club as well as all the first class passengers. On this day, that was around 12 people. She said he is great to fly with because he really treats the passengers AND the crew very well, mentioning that he had brought scones to all of them that morning.

I fly A LOT. In the last 20 years, I've probably traveled on over 800 flights all around the world. In that time, I've never received a personal note from the Captain.

Entrepreneurs and major corporations alike can learn from this story. Personal service that goes above and beyond the call of duty, can generate great word of mouth.

Captain Fletcher – my hat's off to you. Well done. I think this is a great example of how one person in a really large company can make a difference in a customer's attitude. Your note was creative and appreciated. I hope to be flying with you again.

5. The Follow Up call is a little thing that makes a big difference [PG #365]

From Barry Dalton of Customer Service Stories. Barry referenced a post from Kristina Evey. {Endnote 109}

Here is an excerpt from Kristina:

> *I love being a mom more than anything else in the whole world, even chocolate. But, one of the things I dread as a mom is getting that phone call from school informing me that one of my children has "Pinkeye." So, last Tuesday, I picked up my daughter from school and headed to the doctor's office for the diagnosis that I already knew was coming and then to the drug store to pick up the prescription drops.*

Now, putting drops into the eyes of a six year old is no easy feat. Especially when that six year old has decided that she is a drama queen and is going to milk the situation for all it is worth. When I picked up the drops, the pharmacist at Rite Aid suggested some methods for administering the drops that might make it easier and less stressful. Nonetheless, the suggested methods were just as torturous as me literally sitting on my daughter and squirting the drops in her eyes.

However, after two days of drops every four hours, my daughter and I came to a point where we did try the pharmacist's suggestion and were able to administer the drops with no drama at all. So, this is a pretty mundane situation. Nothing really noteworthy.

Until... we get the call from the pharmacist two days later asking how my daughter's eye infection is doing and if we had any problems administering the eye drops. No, this wasn't a call from the doctor's office. It was the pharmacist from Rite Aid delivering excellent customer service. She was taking the time and interest to call and see how the treatment was working, if we had encountered any problems, and if we had any questions she could answer. She was connecting with me, the customer. The business transaction, for all practical purposes, was complete. She was following up to nurture the relationship. That's effectively managing the customer experience. Now, they may have designed this into the process at Rite Aid. But that's the point – they design a positive customer experience into their plans.

This really might not seem like a big deal, until you think about how often this doesn't happen. How many times do you receive a follow up phone call from the provider of the product or service you purchased from to see if there was anything they could help you with? I'll bet it's less often than you think.

The noticeable thing is that it wasn't the physician who treated her, or even that office. I paid them much more for the physician's time and diagnosis than I did the drug store for the drops.

Customer satisfaction comes from the extra step that we put on to our delivery of service. I was happy just to leave the pharmacy with the drops I needed and the fact that they were nice and pleasant to me. I'm delighted that they called to follow up. Even though I know I may pay a little more to go to Rite Aid, the fact that I received that follow up call tells me they care about my business.

Marketing Lagniappe Takeaway: We've seen the follow up call cited a few times in the Project. It's a smart move for the following reasons:

1. Demonstrates you care – The transaction isn't over when money is exchanged. It shows the customer that you are concerned about their satisfaction.
2. Low cost – This is something that can be done by the pharmacist or business owner during a lull in the ordinary course of business.
3. Troubleshooting – The vast majority of people will not complain. Following up allows you to correct any service issues and extend the life of your customer relationships.

6. Making it Personal [PG #438]

Capital Grill provides personalized cards from the servers. They make an effort to get to know their customers. They want you to build a relationship with your server.

7. Playing the right cards [PG #476]

Submitted by James Sorensen:

My aunt recently required outpatient surgery at Advocate Lutheran General Hospital in Park Ridge. When my aunt and I arrived we were greeted by a receptionist with a smile, met with the insurance coordinator who thoroughly explained the insurance coverage, spoke with the nurse that took extra time to make sure my aunt was comfortable and finally the doctor whom she has grown to trust over the years.

After the surgery, when I arrived to pick up my aunt, a volunteer from the hospital was waiting in front with her and graciously helped her into my car. We stopped by a local restaurant for lunch and my aunt showed me her discharge paperwork along with a card that read "I hope your visit today was excellent." I thought to myself that's nice gesture, but a big surprise awaited us when my aunt opened the card and found it was hand signed by people she was in contact with that day.

What a great example of how the health-care system is utilizing unique ways of reaching out to their patients by showing compassion and delivering a memorable experience.

8. A little proactive extra [PG #593]

Submitted to the Purple Goldfish Project via tweet by Paul Tracy.

In Paul's words:

> *OK, I have to admit that I've been a fan of Shui Tea for some time. I don't even remember how I stumbled across his website or why I made my first order from Shui Tea. Maybe it was the subtly irreverent attitude of the purveyor that just meshed with my personality or the product descriptions on the website.*

> *Regardless, I've been really happy with the quality of the tea that I've ordered from him and have placed a few orders. I'm relatively new to tea, but have been recording my tea reviews on this website called Steepster for a few months. I tend to be brutally truthful and in all honesty, I have really enjoyed everything I have ordered from Shui Tea.*

> *Today, I received an e-mail from the owner of Shui Tea that had, in part, the following: "I wanted to thank you for sharing so much about Shui Tea on Steepster and online. I just put a $10 store credit on your account to use if you order again. No expiration, and feel free to use it anytime and with other*

coupons you might see in e-mails or on Twitter." I took advantage of the generous offer immediately because there were already a number of new items from Shui Tea that I wanted to try.

The whole purpose of this post is to point out what a customer service and marketing genius the owner of Shui Tea has revealed himself to be. I was already a devoted fan of his brand. Through a very short and simple, yet personal, contact he has secured a customer for life. If there are ever any issues in the future (which I don't expect but can happen) I'll be more than willing to forgive them given the treatment he's afforded me to date.

In business, providing superb customer service and delivering lagniappe is like putting money into the bank. You are building up credit with your customers. As Paul alluded to above, if and when an issue arises you will be given leeway due to the goodwill you've earned.

9. Know Your Customers [PG #336]
Marty Desmond left this example within a comment on Kelly Ketelboeter's post, "What is Your Purple Goldfish?" {Endnote 110}

Gumba's in Sunnyvale, CA

I went for breakfast with friends at one of our favorite places on Saturday. We sat outdoors for the first time since street construction began months ago. As we were served, I watched how much fun the employees were having. I told my friends that it was great seeing the restaurant busy again and that I knew the construction hurt much of the business on that block.

I went back Tuesday evening for a quick dinner. As I was eating, the owner came up, patted me on the back and thanked me for my business Saturday morning. Then, he told me how happy he was to see my friends and inquired about them. He asked if the dad had found another job, knowing that he was laid off months ago.

We talked for a few moments more, and then he patted me on the back again, thanked me once more and walked off. I watched him walk away and thought about why I enjoyed that restaurant so much. The food is great, but it's the experience that makes it worth going back.

I realize that no fewer than four of his employees approached my friend to tell them how much they had missed his family. The culture of that business includes personal relationships whenever possible. I think that is a missing ingredient in so many businesses today.

This restaurant has endured six months of lagging sales, due to people wanting to stay away during construction. Yet, they were genuinely concerned about the lives of the people who walked through their doors. To me, every question of "how is your friend" is a purple goldfish.

Chapter 20

#8 - Added Service

"It has long been an axiom of mine that the little things are infinitely the most important."

– Sir Arthur Conan Doyle

AN ADDED TOUCH FOR GOOD MEASURE

The 8th of the 12 types of purple goldfish is an "added service." A little extra service that exceeds the expectations of your customers.

Let's look at eleven examples:

1. Complimentary toner vacuuming [PG #249]

Develop a service that's convenient, good for the environment and saves you money. Then deliver it with a couple purple goldfish. That's the order of the day for the folks at Cartridge World. Here is the example submitted by EJ Kritz:

> To begin, we're in the business of refilling and re-manufacturing printer cartridges. We offer a free delivery service to our business customers during which time plenty of things can happen opening the door for added value.
>
> For example, if we're delivering a cartridge for a laser printer but the businesses fax machine is on the fritz, it's only natural and fitting that we'll do anything we can to help get their fax back up and running. Similarly, many of our franchises keep a "toner vac" in their delivery vehicle. This vacuum is specially designed to handle the fine particles in toner. It's a HUGE benefit to our customers (as silly and small as it sounds) to bring in the toner vac for a complimentary cleaning of their laser printer before we put in

their new cartridge. This service is the printer equivalent of getting a free car wash each time you get a tank of gas... it doesn't help your car run better but it sure does make you feel good.

The last example is something almost universal regardless of which Cartridge World franchise you visit. It's quite simple actually. Each and every business delivery comes complete with a Tootsie Pop. You see, purchasing our product is all about saving money. However, typically the person saving the money (the business owner) is not the same person taking the delivery (the office manager). This little token makes everyone smile in the middle of a busy day! In fact, many of our owners could even tell you the favorite flavor of pop for each of their top customers. Simple, and yes, sweet.

2. Recommending a competitor [PG #397]

Joe Gascoigne, Co-Founder of OnePage cites Zappos:

> *"As for an example, one that springs to mind is that if you try to order shoes from Zappos and they do not have the shoes you want in stock, they will actually recommend a nearby store that does. It seems counter-intuitive, but I think it really builds trust and it obviously works well for them."*

According to an interview with CEO Tony Hsieh in Chief Marketer {Endnote 111}, he refuses to see customer service as an expense. Rather, it's an investment,

> *"Our business is based on repeat customers and word of mouth. There's a lot of value in building up our brand name and what it stands for. We view the money that we spend on customer service as marketing money that improves our brand."*

Here is another great example from an article in *Footwear News*:

According to Jerry Tidmore, who manages Zappos' help-desk concierge service,

> *"One of the craziest stories was that of a customer who checked in to the Mandalay Bay hotel [in nearby Las Vegas] and forgot her shoes."* According to Tidmore, the guest called Zappos, where she had originally purchased the style, looking for a replacement, but they didn't have any in stock. So the company found a pair in the right size at the mall, bought them and delivered them to the hotel — all for free."

3. Just don't exceed expectations . . . obliterate them [PG #493]

Another Zappos example was taken from Peter Osbourne's blog *Bulldog Simplicity*: {Endnote 112}

> *My son lost one of his dress shoes at school the other day. Don't ask. I don't know how you lose one shoe.*
>
> *So last night (Tuesday) he and his mother went to the store where he bought them. Nothing in his size. They get home and for a variety of reasons they don't get online until about 10:00 p.m. They find the shoes and my wife calls Zappos to confirm that we'll get the shoes by Thursday with one-day shipping. I'm not clear on the rest of the conversation, but Zappos waives the overnight delivery charges. No reason*

given, but it sounded like it was because we were first-time buyers.

It's like Tony Hsieh was sitting outside the house when we ordered Tyler's shoes. So we get up this morning to find an e-mail with a tracking number. The doorbell rings at 9 a.m. It's the UPS guy with the shoes. That's right. Eleven hours after ordering the shoes, we had them. The customer survey arrived shortly after delivery, and guess how my wife filled out the score. She's now a customer for life.

Zappos has gotten a lot of great press in recent months and was purchased in July by Amazon, which says it's leaving management in place after the sale closes. Smart man, that Jeff Bezos.

As a first-time buyer, Zappos didn't just exceed our expectations. They obliterated them. And that leaves me with two questions for you, regardless of whether you're a retailer, a consultant, or a person within a large company...

1. When was the last time you obliterated a customer or client's expectations?

2. How can you "Zappos" someone's expectations the next time you deal with them?

[NOTE: Zappos locates their own distribution center next to UPS in Kentucky. They staff the center 24/7/365 which guarantees orders get picked and shipped right away.]

Zappos Marketing Lagniappe Takeaway: Recommending competitors when you don't have the product, hand delivering a pair of shoes and upgrading to overnight shipping... Zappos is a pioneer in ways to proactively add service. Fitting for a shoe company "powered by service" or more appropriately according to Hsieh,

"A customer service company who sells shoes."

4. Splitting sizes, not hairs [PG #667]

It starts with employees. Nordstrom only has one rule...

"Use good judgment in all situations"

It has only one goal...

"To provide outstanding customer service"

This example was taken from a blog post by Ron Kaufman at Up Your Service: {Endnote 113}

> *A sales clerk at Nordstrom in the United States sold my friend a new pair of shoes. Measuring his feet, the clerk discovered my friend's right foot was size 9.5 and the left foot was a smaller 9.0. The clerk gave my friend the shoes he needed to achieve a perfect fit: one 9.5 and the other 9.0. I have no idea what the clerk did with the remaining mismatched shoes, but my friend's loyalty to Nordstrom has been secured. Talk about going above and beyond to improve customer satisfaction!*

I've also experienced this signature lagniappe. Back in 1996 I bought a pair of Dr. Martens at Nordstrom in Portland, Oregon. I distinctly remember the experience, as it was the first time I spent over $100 of my own money on a pair of shoes. Doc's doesn't make half sizes and I couldn't get the right fit between a size 11 and a size 12. My feet are about a 1/2 size apart. The salesperson offered to split the pairs. One word: SOLD.

Marketing Lagniappe Takeaway: Do the unexpected little extra to satisfy your customers. Splitting sizes speaks volumes about Nordstrom's beginnings as a shoe store and its commitment to the customer experience.

5. This one leaves no fingerprints or dust [PG #706]

Safelite was submitted via e-mail by Lee Silverstein:

> *"As I wrote about in my blog post "Adding Value Doesn't Have To Cost A Nickel." {Endnote 114} After replacing your damaged windshield, Safelite AutoGlass cleans ALL of your windows and vacuums the interior of your car. Love your site!"*

Here is Lee's post:

> ### Adding Value Doesn't Have To Cost A Nickel
> *How do you differentiate "good" service from "great" service? You know it when you experience it, but sometimes it's difficult to verbalize. I like to explain the difference as "great" service is the type of service that you would tell others about.*
>
> *You could walk into a store and be cheerfully greeted, but it's unlikely that over dinner that evening you would tell your family about the friendly greeting you received while shopping earlier in the day. Now if that same associate had offered to gift-wrap your purchase and then carried it out to your car for you, then that would be an experience worth sharing. So how do companies, and their employees, take the steps to "make a difference?" By adding value.*
>
> *Making it standard practice to call other locations to find an out-of-stock item adds value to a customer's experience. The car dealer that washes your car when you bring it in for service also adds value. And here's the good news for these businesses: doing these "little things" costs next to nothing!*
>
> *While driving the other day, a pebble hit my windshield, leaving a small crack. I contacted my insurance company, Progressive, and they offered to book an appointment for me to have the windshield replaced the following morning; I was very impressed. As promised, my phone rang shortly after 8 am. It was Rich, from Safelite AutoGlass telling me he was on his way to my home to replace my windshield. After only 45 minutes he called me and asked me to meet him outside; he was finished and needed my signature. I walked outside*

to find him cleaning not just my windshield, but all of my windows! Not only that, but he informed me that he vacuumed the interior of my car as well. By investing 10 extra minutes to vacuum my car and clean my windows, Rich took a good experience and made it a great one. And what did this cost Safelite? Ten minutes of an employees time; a good investment.

6. A personal touch makes all the difference [PG #673]

Jim Joseph, author of *The Experience Effect* {Endnote 115} offers an experience with Lacoste:

I submit to you a great example of amazing customer service that transformed a brand in my mind... the ultimate purple goldfish.

Last summer I was visiting Palm Beach with my son. Just looking to get a little R&R. Some friends who live nearby invited us out for dinner one night, which was great, but I hadn't really packed anything appropriate for my fourteen year old son to wear.

So we went shopping in town, and of course he didn't find anything that he liked .. I figured that I would just make due, and we went back to the pool.

While we were sitting there he remembered a Lacoste shirt that he thought would be perfect. I was thrilled because he rarely cares how he looks and we were going to be visiting friends.

We didn't have a car so we needed to take the hotel shuttle downtown, but I was afraid that we would get there too late. So I called the store only to find out that they were in fact closing for the day.

I guess the person on the other end of the phone could hear the disappointment in my voice, and she asked me what was wrong. Half way through my explanation, she interrupted me

141

to ask me where we were staying. She offered to bring the shirt to us!

So I told her the size and color, which they had in stock, and in fact thirty minutes later she personally pulled up to the hotel to hand deliver the shirt.

That was a wow. Totally made my night, and completely changed my perceptions of the brand. I am now a loyal consumer time and time again, especially for gift giving occasions. Maybe because every time I think of the brand I smile!

Clearly, the brand knows the importance of customer service in the total experience and has made sure that they deliver on it at the store level. A true purple goldfish!

7. Fast, Casual and now High Touch [PG #581]

This example comes courtesy of Jennifer Phelps. In Jenn's words:

> "Boston Market gives kids balloons (which is nice). They also hand carry your tray to your table which is helpful."

Boston Market turned 25 in 2010. It looks like they are revamping both their offerings and service model. According to seriouseats.com, {Endnote 116}

> *Boston Market is giving its restaurants something of a makeover. 370 of their nearly 500 locations will be revamped by the end of 2010, with the stores in the Miami and New York markets leading the charge. Some of the changes are small, some are large. The side orders in the "Hot Case" will be cooked in smaller pots, so the food is prepared more frequently, and less is wasted. They are increasing staff, and will have employees escorting customers to their tables, as well as bussing the tables after they're finished. Finally, and most interestingly, Boston Market is introducing real plates and silverware for dine-in guests—bringing the experience away from the traditional tray-to-table fast-food model.*

The renovations can be summed up by Tony Buford, Senior Vice President – Operations,

> *"We are proud of our new offering but it's more than just paint, pots and poultry – it's the people. The people are the heart and soul of the company, and what makes Boston Market America's kitchen table."*

Kudos to Boston Market for raising their game and focusing on customer experience.

8. Service that flies into the Purple Goldfish Project [PG #300]

Submitted by Brian Millman:

> *I wanted to send through a Purple Goldfish to help in your quest for 1,001. I'm not sure if you have heard of Porter Airlines, but it is a short-haul airline which flies out of Toronto's city centre airport (very cute and small airport) and focuses on business travelers. It started primarily operating in Canada with one US route to Newark but has expanded to fly to Boston, Chicago and Myrtle Beach.*

> *With most airlines, you expect to sit in the typical terminal with old rows of seats. At Porter's hub, they offer a VIP lounge for everyone. The terminal area is set up similar to that of any VIP lounge: a kitchen stocked filled with FREE soda and water, two cappuccino machines, and free snacks (Cookies & chips). Porter also offers FREE Wi-Fi with a power port under every seat as well as 14 computers for those without a laptop.*

> *ALSO- not sure if I have gotten lucky, but supposedly there is an $100 change fee for jumping on an earlier flight… but I haven't been charged for it once.*

9. This Purple Goldfish is easy to write up [PG #401]

Salute from Peter Hurley of Synergy Events.

> "Had lunch today at Salute in New York City (270 Madison Ave). Nice upscale restaurant that caters to a business crowd. Upon sitting at the table I noticed a purple goldfish. Each table came with a tiny notepad similar to those you would get at a conference or hotel. It was for notes if needed during lunch. The small pad was branded with Salute's marks and contact info. A nice little keepsake compliments of the restaurant."

Marketing Lagniappe Takeaway: Embrace the purpose of your clientele. If they are dining to conduct business, figure out ways like a little notepad to grease the wheels of commerce.

10. It's always 5 o'clock [PG #78]

Horizon Air was submitted by Marcia Hoover:

> "The best one I can think of is Horizon Air – the regional affiliate for Alaska Airlines. They have always served free beer and wine to all passengers on their flights. Given today's economy and stifling service in the airline industry Horizon definitely stands out as a marketing lagniappe."

11. What's Your Thermometer? [PG #664]

From Ron Kaufman at *Up Your Service* {Endnote 117}:

> "A waiter at La Pirogue Resort in Mauritius comes to work each day with a thermometer in his pocket. On the way to the restaurant he takes the temperature of the ocean water and the swimming pool. As he pours coffee and clears plates during breakfast, he joyfully tells guests exactly how warm and enjoyable their swimming will be that day. What a great way to improve customer satisfaction!

Chapter 21

#9 - Waiting

"The secret to success is to treat all customers as if your world revolves around them."

-Unknown

WE SPEND 10% OF OUR LIFE WAITING...

The 9th of the 12 types of purple goldfish is all about "waiting". Waiting for your customers is inevitable, especially if you are a successful business. How you handle those moments and the little extras you offer can make a big difference.

Enough waiting already, let's look at eight examples:

1. Ugh... Flight Delays [PG #414]

JetBlue flies in from Sharon Trainor-Smith. Sharon talks about an experience with the airline:

> *When flights are delayed they often show up at the gate with tables full of free water and snacks, and then set up a trivia game for everyone with good prizes such as free flight tickets, gift certificates, etc. The stranded passengers LOVED these bonuses and there was a lot of positive buzz. Plus by giving out flight tickets, we were incentivized to come back to JetBlue. It turned a bad situation into a really positive group and brand bonding opportunity.*

Marketing Lagniappe Takeaway: When faced with lemons... make lemonade. Make the best out of a bad situation by being proactive. It's not about the water, snacks or trivia... it's about what they represent. They stand for the fact you care about your customers. Kudos to JetBlue for bringing a little humanity back to air travel.

2. Smart moves that make waiting less painful [PG #509]

They say (whoever "*they*" are) that we spend 10% of our life waiting. Even with all the practice we get, waiting still is painful. If you are a business prone to peak throughput, you take steps to make the waiting bearable.

This example of Great Wolf Lodge was taken from Connecticut Magazine {Endnote 118}:

> "*At peak check in times the lodge has a face painter, juggler and balloon sculptor wandering to entertain guests.*"

3. Peanuts become a tasty diversion to waiting [PG #94]

Five Guys Burgers and Fries is one of my favorite waiting examples of 'marketing lagniappe'. There is a huge box when you walk in. In the early days the long lines forced Jerry Murrell and his sons to distribute free, unshelled peanuts to placate waiting customers. The peanuts have become a FIVE GUYS trademark.

4. Put your name on the pad and grab a glass of complimentary wine [PG #143]

Pacific Cafe, a seafood restaurant in San Francisco, offers free glasses of wine while you wait for a table. They don't accept reservations and it's a popular spot, so the beverage is a nice gesture to extend to patrons as they wait to be seated.

5. It's 'all about' the fans of your brand [PG #503]

Lady Gaga was tweeted into the Project by Tim Baran (@uMCLE):

Here is an excerpt by TJ from Neon Limelight: {Endnote 119}

> *Say what you will about Lady Gaga... her persona is over the top; her music videos are blasphemous — but one thing you can never say is that she doesn't love her fans (Little Monsters).*

Her connection with her Little Monsters is undeniable and the lengths she'll go to prove that are boundless.

Several Gaga fans camped out in early July in front of the Rockefeller Plaza and braved the scorching New York City heat a day ahead of her concert appearance on the Today Show to ensure they got a prime spot.

Once Gaga learned that her Little Monsters were going all out to see her perform, she sprung into action to make sure the wait was a bit more bearable. "My little monster sweeties are already camped outside today show! I love u! Will be sending u pizza and water all day!" she tweeted.

6. Raising the bar on CX when faced with steep demand [PG #391]

This story featuring ABT Electronics was taken from post entitled, "It's the Customer Experience, Stupid" {Endnote 120} from Ryan Deutsch of StrongMail:

At its core, it is the customer experience that turns a one-time buyer into a loyal customer, subscriber, fan or follower. I feel we lose sight of this fact at times. I had an experience last month that reminded me how true loyalty is created between a brand and a consumer.

For those of you unaware, the federal government in the state of Illinois offered $6.5 million in rebates to consumers who purchased "Energy Saver" appliances between April 15 and April 25. Not being one to pass up money from the government, I rushed to ABT Electronics in Glenview. Our family was in desperate need of a new microwave oven. As I walked into ABT, it became clear that this was no ordinary sale. They had parking attendants directing traffic and the store was an absolute madhouse. I was immediately dejected assuming there was no chance of finding an associate to help me, let alone make a purchase. I found the microwave section and stood there looking lost for no more *than 90 seconds before a young woman approached and asked if she could help.*

"Yes, which microwaves qualify for the energy saver government rebate?"

She looked at me and admitted she had no idea and ran (yes, literally ran) down the aisle towards a manager and started speaking. After about 15 seconds, she ran (yes, literally ran) back to me and explained that microwaves were not part of the government rebate program. While I appreciated her enthusiasm, I was less than happy. But I still needed a microwave, so I asked what she knew about combination microwave/convection ovens. Again she knew little but promised to find someone who did and off she went.

Less than two minutes had passed when a gentleman in a General Electric golf shirt walked up to me and said: "I hear you need help with microwaves."

Now this was impressive. The store was mobbed, and in less than 90 seconds, I had an actual GE employee answering questions about GE appliances. A real subject matter expert on hand to help me! ABT had their vendors bring in experts to help customers understand the benefits of various appliances for the sales event. In less than two minutes, this gentleman helped me decide on a microwave oven, and I had forgotten all about the lack of the government rebate. The GE employee handed me off to a man in an ABT vest: "Follow me," he said and off we went towards a line that must have included 700 people. My eyes rolled back in my head and I said, "Listen maybe this wasn't the best day to come in…"

He cut me off, saying, "Don't worry, we will be done in less than five minutes."

Sure enough, this guy found a computer terminal and had me checked out in no time. I was in and out of the store on the busiest day of its existence in less than 30 minutes, feeling great about the product I purchased, even without the government discount.

Halfway to the exit my wife called. "Ryan, can you do me a favor and buy that replacement filter for our refrigerator?" she asked.

"Aargh," was my response. I explained, "Rachel this place is crazy! There's no way I'm going to be able to find a replacement filter." I could feel my wife rolling her eyes — she's been trying to get me to order this filter for more than two months.

"OK," I finally said. At that moment a different gentleman in an ABT vest walked past. "Excuse me, sir," I said. "Do you guys sell replacement filters for your refrigerators?" We both looked toward the refrigerator section, which was a zoo. The refrigerators were actually included in the government rebate program. "You know what," I said. "Don't worry about it. I'll come back another time."

"No, no that's silly," the gentleman said. "I'll take care of you." And off we went in search of a computer terminal. The gentleman started flipping his fingers across the keyboard and asked me a few questions.

He then said, "I apologize if this takes a few minutes to process your order, I am the CFO, so bear with me." My jaw hit the floor.

Here I am at ABT on the biggest day of the year and the CFO is helping me make a $44 purchase. Not only did he treat me as if I were the most important person in the store, this guy, the CFO, was capable of entering an order into a computer terminal on the store floor and selling somebody something. I was absolutely blown away and walked out of there completely committed to buying every future electronic appliance from ABT.

In addition to my loyalty, thanks to the wonder of the social web, I took the time to write this blog talking about my experience at their store. Once finished with it, I will post it to my Twitter account, my LinkedIn page and hopefully one or two of the blogs I contribute to on a regular basis, sharing the story with thousands more readers. The blogs will deliver

149

the story via email to an even broader audience. I am already a subscriber to ABT's email communications, and I will continue to anticipate and appreciate those communications.

The point here is that customer loyalty does not start on a Facebook page or in a Twitter feed. It is not developed solely through relevant email communications and the appropriate cadence of messages.

Engagement between a brand and a consumer in any channel (email or social media) starts with the customer's experience with that brand. If the customer experience is average, your consumer is unlikely to be a repeat buyer, they are less likely to click and open your communications, and they are never going to spend their social capital recruiting their friends to be your customers.

This is a tremendous story on so many levels. First – let's look at the quad purple goldfishes:

1. Parking attendants in the lot directing traffic. Great first impression.
2. Quick service that gets quicker. Love the running bit.
3. Making checkout painless and fast.
4. Senior management that dives into the trenches and terminals.

Ryan really hits the nail on the head. It all starts with the customer experience and going above and beyond for your customers. Loyalty isn't gained via a Facebook page, a Twitter feed or an e-mail campaign. The net effect is the generation of positive word of mouth. You effectively give your customer something to talk, tweet, Facebook and blog about. Ryan does exactly that and more.

7. H2O while you wait [PG #625]

J.Crew flows into the Purple Goldfish Project courtesy of a submission by Jim Joseph, author of *The Experience Effect*

So here's another purple goldfish, and I actually feature it in my book... I experienced it again yesterday.

J.Crew. I'm a huge fan, have been a for awhile. Brand experience is exceptional, always consistent whether you are at the store, online, or browsing the category. Distinct to each of those venues, but always J.Crew.

The shopping experience in store is particularly good. The sales staff all wear the clothing, so you can actually see how things will look. I've had many of them show me how to tie a tie the "just so cool way" they are wearing them, or how to role the cuffs up on a pair of jeans, or how to partner a pair of shoes with new khakis. This is in store, but they also offer a personal shopping service online as well.

I was at one of the Manhattan stores yesterday, and as you can imagine for a Saturday afternoon in December it was packed. Didn't matter though, the service was impeccable. When I walked in the door, I was greeted by a salesperson. I immediately told her that I was looking for a purple jacket for my daughter... she immediately took me to the back of the store to see three options. I went upstairs to the mens department where the service was just as good, despite the crowds.

With merchandise in hand, I proceeded to the registers where there was a huge long line. Here's the kicker... more sales people were working the line with buckets of small bottles of water for the people who were waiting. They also helped select more items while people were in line.

That's a purple goldfish!

8. Spa services included [PG #628]

Submitted via e-mail from Carolyn Ray. She nominates Purple Goldfish Hall of Famer Lexus:

Survey Questions

We invite you to enjoy a Complimentary Spa Amenity while your vehicle is being serviced. Take your choice:

☐ Complimentary Manicure ☐ Complimentary Pedicure
☐ Complimentary Teeth Whitening ☐ Complimentary Haircut
☐ Complimentary Blowdry ☐ Complimentary Fitness Center Session

> *"At Lexus of North Miami, people who come in for service are entitled to a complimentary spa service {Endnote 121} at their in house spa. Services include manicures, pedicures, haircuts, waxing or chair massage. There is a full service cafe, kids playroom, fitness center and pool room for waiting customers. Makes coming in for service a total pleasure!"*

Marketing Lagniappe Takeaway: If you are going to make people wait... figure out ways to make the waiting more bearable. If you are a leader like Lexus, you give your dealerships carte blanche to create experiences that customers actually look forward to. Lexus gets it and utilizes the "little extras" as a key differentiator in the car ownership experience.

Chapter 22

#10 - Convenience

"We see our customers as invited guests
to a party, and we are the hosts.
It's our job every day to make every important aspect
of the customer experience a little bit better."
-Jeff Bezos

EASY PEASY... GEORGE AND WEEZY

The 10th of the 12 types of purple goldfish surrounds the idea of "convenience". A little unexpected extra that makes things easier.

Let's look at 7 examples:

1. Ice, Ice Baby [PG #22]

Simple, yet an effective and noteworthy little extra. Whole Foods enters the Purple Goldfish Project from Claire Gallo:

> *"I live in West Hartford, CT. When you shop at Whole Foods and buy fish, meat or poultry... the folks at Whole Foods will offer to give you ice for free. Very nice touch, especially if you have other errands or plan to shop around town."*

2. Find the stuffed animal [PG #320]

Jody Padar submits Trader Joe's:

> *"The stuffed whale that hides at Trader Joe's. If you find him, your child gets a treat out of a treasure box. Then you get to re-hide him. My kids love to go to Trader Joe's to find the stuffed animal. It keeps them entertained while shopping. Hint: He spends a lot of time in the snack food isle."*

3. Miniature shopping carts for the kids [PG #591]

Trader Joe's submitted by Jennifer Phelps:

> "TJ's has kid-sized shopping carts. Great way to keep our two boys busy when we go shopping. They get such a kick out of pushing their own carts."

Trader Joe's was originally submitted to the Project by Amy DeRobertis. In Amy's words:

> "There's a fun theme going on here — from Giuseppe Joe's to Trader Jose's, the notion of no middle man is seen on its product labels as well as in the mentality of its Hawaiian shirt wearing associates. And the ongoing bevy of free samples at its dedicated sampling stations keeps you interested in the constantly evolving choices and happy rather than devastated when your favorite entree goes missing. There's bound to be something just as great coming down the pike."

Kudos to TJ's for thinking about the little things for the little ones . . . convenience makes a big difference.

4. Repel clamshell casings and wire ties [PG #165]

Submitted by Adam Brett:

> "Amazon's frustrating free packaging is a brilliant idea. I'm sure having little ones you have battled the wires before trying to open up a gift."

[Notes on the Packaging: The Certified Frustration-Free Package is recyclable and comes without excess packaging materials such as hard plastic clamshell casings, plastic bindings, and wire ties. It's designed to be opened without the use of a box cutter or knife and will protect your product just as well as traditional packaging. Products with Frustration-Free Packaging can frequently be shipped in their own boxes, without an additional shipping box.]

5. Reaping the rewards of convenience [PG #716]

Submitted by James Mayer, a fellow brother from America's oldest professional business fraternity *Alpha Kappa Psi*. He recommended TD Bank via a post from Jim Taggart at the blog *Changing Winds*: {Endnote 122}

Here is an excerpt:

> As [CEO Ed] Clark expressed in an interview with the *Financial Post Magazine*:
>
>> The great thing about our model is if I put a branch on a corner in New York City, I know five years later I will have more than 25% of the local business, because at some time in that five years someone will come by at 4:02 pm. Their branch will be closed, they'll look across at our store, this beautiful store, there will be someone giving dog biscuits to somebody's dog, they'll walk in and there's a greeter that's unbelievably friendly, and they'll say, 'So why am I banking at the guy across the street?'
>>
>> On Sundays we send our bankers out to all the small businesses and say, "You're open, we're open, and you bank with the bank that's closed. It's a very simple concept: Just be open longer and give better service." Clark also noted, for example, that their branch at 2 Wall Street, which opened five years ago, now has $1 billion in deposits.

Marketing Lagniappe Takeaway: Be open, convenient and give better service. Words to live by.

6. Curbside service makes pick-up a drive by [PG #306]

Submitted by Jack Campisi:

> Thai Basil in Greenwich, CT is a Purple Goldfish. Not only do they have great Thai food, but excellent service as well.
>
> Their lagniappe is the curbside pick-up. They are located on a busy and crowed stretch of road in downtown Greenwich. Parking at dinner time can be a nightmare, and could prevent you from even attempting take-out. Well, have no

fear. You can give them your credit card number when you place your order and then give them a call when you are pulling up to the restaurant.

You pullover and they will run out, hand you your food through your window and let you sign your receipt right in your car. And they always do it with a big smile. In no time you are back home, enjoying a nice meal. (If you go and you like some heat, try the Spicy Fried Rice)

Marketing Lagniappe Takeaway: Thai Basil understands the importance of access and convenience when take-out is concerned. Here they've turned a bad parking situation into a positive by running out with the food and your receipt. A little something extra indeed.

7. Purple Goldfish Swim in Schools [PG #464]

A school of purple goldfish in the Project comes courtesy of Dan Oltersdorf at Campus Advantage.

As a former RA (both in undergrad and in graduate school) I especially like number one. Anything you can do to make move in easier goes a long way.

Taken from his blog post, {Endnote 123} here is Dan's contribution:

Thanks to @barrymoltz, I just read the @9INCHMarketing ebook: "In Search of Your Purple Goldfish" by Stan Phelps. It is brief and it is worth the read. Unlike my "Puking Baby Policy", the concept of a Purple Goldfish is something that CAN be proceduralized. In fact, that is a key ingredient. A Purple Goldfish is something every customer gets…

I won't try to give you the entire concept, but in essence, the "purple goldfish" is something above and beyond that you consistently give to your customer that sets you apart.

Think of Southwest (your bags fly free), the warm cookies you get every time you check into a DoubleTree Hotel, or for those of you who have ordered from Zappos, their VIP upgrade with free overnight shipping after your second order.

Phelps contends there is no such thing as "meeting expectations" in customer service anymore. We either fail to meet expectations, or we exceed them. Meeting them is a thing of the past and it is NOT ENOUGH.

Read the eBook {Endnote 124} and think about what your purple goldfish are. Here are some ideas from some Campus Advantage properties to get you started:

1. Move-ins… Having cold water and snacks in the apartments for people as they are moving in. Having a dedicated staff member during the move-ins whose job is simply to hand out ice pops on a hot day.
2. Door to door package delivery… instead of making residents come to the front desk, we deliver packages to them at their room or apartment
3. Milk & cookie carts during finals week
4. Every team member, from CA to porter to GM provides a friendly greeting 100% of the time to any person we encounter on a property, prospect or resident
5. Concierge booklet at the front desk with everything from pizza delivery numbers to who to call if you are struggling in your physics class.

These are just a few to get you started… ask yourself, what will stand out? What will people tell stories about?

What else are you doing that qualifies as a "purple goldfish?" What else SHOULD you be doing that will make you stand out.

Chapter 23

#11 - Special Needs

*"Be everywhere, do everything,
and never fail to astonish the customer."*

- Macy's Motto

THE EXTRAS FOR THOSE WHO REQUIRE A LITTLE EXTRA

The 11th of the 12 types of purple goldfish involves handling "special needs." A little unexpected extra to help your customers who need extra care or attention.

Let's look at 7 examples:

1. Thoughtful and proactive for a customer in need [PG #656]

Taken from a post by Ty Sullivan {Endnote 125} of Cafe Metro:

> *While running one of our contests on a gloomy rainy morning, I noticed one of our followers had posted a picture of herself with the Tweet message saying, "Does this look sad enough?" Curious, I tweeted her, "Not doing the contest today? Why so blue?"*
>
> *Turns out her father had passed away the day before and she was unable to return home to attend the funeral due to finances. I had remembered that at one point she had tweeted us questioning why we didn't carry Honey Nut Cheerios as a cereal selection as is it was her favorite. So I called the store she ordered from regularly and had the manager check her order history to see what she enjoyed ordering on a regular basis.*

From there, we created a small gift basket with her favorite lunch and snacks and right in the center, a box of Honey Nut Cheerios and delivered it to her that morning.

She was so overwhelmed with gratitude she could not stop talking about us on Twitter and even came by the store to hug our manager.

2. Taking care of a loyal customer [PG #364]

Submitted by Jed Langdon from a comment on the post, "What's Your Purple Goldfish?" by Kelly Ketelboeter: {Endnote 126}

Hi Kelly. I promised a Purple Goldfish and here it is, sorry it has taken so long!

My girlfriend's father is a HUGE Pizza Express fan and I can now understand why. I'm not sure if you have Pizza Express in the US, but in the UK it is a large Pizza restaurant franchise with over 300 restaurants in the UK (it is called Pizza Marzano in some other countries). He visits his local Pizza Express on average about once a fortnight and is on first name terms with a lot of the staff there. When he walks in the chef usually begins to make his favourite dish, but what is even more impressive is that this is a starter that is no longer on the menu. This is a relationship that has been built up over time through him visiting the restaurant and not because he knows any of the staff, which is often the reason for a customer getting this treatment.

Anyway, a couple of weeks ago, my girlfriend's father was admitted to hospital (fortunately he is going to be OK) and on hearing about him being in hospital the manager of his local Pizza Express took it upon herself to surprise him with his favourite pizza! She contacted the Pizza Express which was closest to the hospital and asked them to make and deliver the pizza to the hospital, free of charge. This is one of the kindest and most generous acts I have seen from a business, and nobody had expected this sort of thought and effort. Talk about making a customer feel valued, special and delivering service way above and beyond expectations!

Another great post Kelly, keep up the brilliant work!

Marketing Lagniappe Takeaway: Go above and beyond to help a loyal customer in need.

3. Allergy friendly becomes a differentiator [PG #690]

Sarah Gore of STANCE shared an article in the *New York Times* {Endnote 127} on Hypoallergenic Hotel Rooms at the Hyatt and Fairmont chains.

Here is an excerpt from the article by Tara Mohn:

Sneeze Free Zone

Even die-hard road warriors need a comfortable place to recharge after a long day. But for business travelers with allergies, asthma and other sensitivities, hotel rooms can be rife with dust mites, mold, animal dander and other allergens that set off sneezing, itchy eyes, headaches and sleepless nights.

Individual hotels have long accommodated guests by cleaning rooms with special products and processes and washing linens in hot water with no or fragrance-free detergent. They have also offered mattress and pillow protectors, rugless rooms and windows that open.

But now, two hotel chains, Hyatt Hotels and Resorts and Fairmont Hotels and Resorts, are taking the service even further by designating permanent allergy-friendly rooms, with things like medical-grade air purifiers and chemical- and fragrance-free bath products.

Thirty-eight percent of hotels offer some kind of allergy-friendly service in guest rooms, a 14 percent increase in the last two years, according to the 2010 Lodging Survey prepared for the American Hotel and Lodging Association by STR, a hotel research company.

Hyatt recently announced plans to create hypoallergenic rooms in all of its full-service hotels in North America. The rooms, which will soon total about 2,000 in 125 properties, cost $20 to $30 extra a night and are intended to eliminate up to 98 percent of allergens and irritants. A medical-grade purifier continuously circulates air, Hyatt said.

"This was a market really underserved," said Tom Smith, vice president of rooms for Hyatt.

The number of allergy sufferers is believed to have gone up substantially since the late '70s, said Dr. Darryl Zeldin, senior investigator and acting clinical director of the National Institute of Environmental Health Sciences. Roughly half of Americans are sensitive to at least one common allergen. Different testing methods may account for some of the increase, but better hygiene resulting in less exposure to bacteria is also thought to play a role, Dr. Zeldin said.

Brian Brault, chief executive of Pure Solutions, the company that installs and maintains Hyatt's hypoallergenic rooms, said more than 200 hotels nationwide, including properties at several major brands, had Pure Solutions rooms, but Hyatt was the first to offer them across its brands. Some hotel conference centers also use the technology, he said.

Lisa Abbott, a marketing consultant for nonprofit groups in Oakland, Calif., who suffers from multiple chemical sensitivities, has learned the benefits firsthand of good air quality in a hotel room.

At home, she rarely takes the morning rush hour train, to avoid "breathing in a soup of fumes and fragrances" from deodorant, hair products and freshly laundered clothing. Traveling, she said, has "always been dicey." But she stayed in one of Hyatt's new rooms on a recent trip to Chicago. "The air is purer," she said. "I slept great. I felt energized both

162

days of conferences. It has just completely opened up my travel options."

Marketing Lagniappe Takeaway: Differentiate yourself by offering that little extra. It doesn't have to be a "throw-in." You can go the extra mile and charge a premium for the added value.

4. Going above and beyond for those with special dietary issues [PG #684]

Taken from a blog post by Hank Davis {Endnote 128} at the SALT & Pepper Group:

> *Faye and I are both pretty big fans of having others do the cooking for us. We eat out a lot and we also order in quite a bit. We experience food service customer service on a very personal level. Unfortunately for Faye, her food allergies make dining out a sometimes, terrible experience. She cannot have anything dairy and she cannot even come close to anything from the onion family. She cannot even have something that has touched a grill that has had an onion on it. This makes things really tough.*
>
> *Recently, however, the team at The Rainforest Cafe made it not so tough for her. In fact, they went above and beyond to the point Faye could not wait to get home from her lunch date with a friend to share the great story with me. Here are the five things that happened that absolutely blew her away and made her day at The Rainforest Cafe.*
>
> > o *At The Rainforest Cafe Faye did not have to volunteer her allergies to the server because the server started off with a great question: "does anybody have any food allergies we should know about?" She did this with a smile and genuine concern for her guests. Typically, Faye has to initiate an awkward and sometimes uncomfortable conversation about her allergies but not at The Rainforest Cafe.*

163

- At The Rainforest Cafe her server actually pointed out, with great care and concern, some specific meal options that might match up with her allergies. She made some really good suggestions which, in our experience, is rare.

- At The Rainforest Cafe the server brought out a separate menu that covered many of the allergy concerns that many of their guests have. This was great and made Faye feel pretty special.

- At The Rainforest Cafe the head chef came out of the kitchen to say hello, introduce himself and see if he could help in any way. He guided Faye through their lunch options, made several specific suggestions and then hand delivered her meal to her after it was prepared. After the meal he came back to check to see how she liked it.

- At The Rainforest Cafe the team took it as a challenge to delight and please my better half and that makes me a Raving Fan (shout out to Ken Blanchard) of The Rainforest Cafe. They loved what they were doing and it made us love their company.

The bottom line is this: I am talking positively about The Rainforest Cafe, I am planning on going to The Rainforest Cafe again and I am very thankful to The Rainforest Cafe for making Faye's Day. When she is happy, I am happy and she was definitely happy.

Great work and thank you!

Marketing Lagniappe Takeaway: Concerns like food allergies are no small matter to your customer. Go above and beyond to proactively address concerns and demonstrate you care.

5. Adding a personal touch [PG #685]

Taken from a tweet by @jenniferpbrown:

> *"Sherrie at #Marriott is a rockstar. Remembered I was worried abt waking up on time. Called me herself to make sure I was awake. #custserv"*

6. Sweetness for the final approach [PG #780]

Submitted by @sjlz:

> *"@9INCHmarketing @jackcampisi you guys probably have this #purplegoldfish but the 'sweets for landing' at Virgin Atlantic help your ears pop!"*

7. Here's the Rub: Invest in Your Customers and Watch Your Business Grow [PG #343]

Submitted by Jake Hillman:

> *My wife, Sabina, owns Body Evolution Massage and Wellness Center. As a massage therapist, her basic job is to help people relax and feel better. What most people do not expect is her knack for the unexpected: coming in on Sunday's to accommodate a client's schedule; sending home remedies to support healing, often at her expense; calling the next day to follow-up and find out how someone is feeling. Her clientele has grown not from common marketing, but from uncommon service, care and connection.*

Marketing Lagniappe Takeaway: I like the phrase *"uncommon marketing."* This type of personal touch beyond the transaction is an investment in your business. It shows you care and spurs customer loyalty.

Chapter 24

#12 - Handling Mistakes

*"Customers don't expect you to be perfect. They do expect
you to fix things when they go wrong."*

-Donald Porter

NOBODY IS PERFECT, NOT EVEN A PERFECT STRANGER

The last type of purple goldfish will seem like an odd addition to the list. In business we are generally conditioned to never admit failure. Let's face it... we all make mistakes. How you deal with them is the real question. It's important to not only correct the problem, but to go above and beyond to make things right.

The idea of proactively admitting to mistakes is totally unexpected. Admit your wrongdoing, ask the customer what they'd like as amends and then always exceed their request. This is brilliant on so many levels. First, it is Dale Carnegie-esque... admit when you're wrong and do it emphatically. It takes the steam out of a complaint. Second, it involves the customer as part of the solution. Let them be judge and jury. This speaks volumes about your willingness to make things right. Lastly, you exceed the proposed solution. Within reason you take the solution and notch it up one or two levels. This gets back to the idea of being totally unexpected.

Let's look at four examples:

1. When you are wrong . . . [PG #438]

Nurse Next Door comes from the book *'Customer Love:'* {Endnote 129}

"Humble Pie. When this Canadian home health care service provider stumbles... they deliver a fresh baked apple pie and a note apologizing for poor customer service. Each year they spend about $1,500 on pies, but they estimate it saves about $100,000 in business going elsewhere. That sounds like pretty strong ROI as over 70% of customers that take their business elsewhere do so because of poor customer service."

Marketing Lagniappe Takeaway: When you're wrong... admit it and make amends quickly.

2. A $1.6 million dollar oops [PG #407]

I came across a post on Inside Zappos {Endnote 130} via a tweet by 'The Experience Factor' @jenkuhnpr:

> *Hey everyone – As many of you may know (and I'm sure a lot of you do not), 6pm.com is our sister site. 6pm.com is where brandaholics go for their guilt free daily fix of the brands they crave. Every day, the site highlights discounts on products ranging up to 70% off. Well, this morning, we made a big mistake in our pricing engine that capped*

everything on the site at $49.95. The mistake started at midnight and went until around 6:00 a.m. When we figured out the mistake was happening, we had to shut down the site for a bit until we got the pricing problem fixed.

While we're sure this was a great deal for customers, it was inadvertent, and we took a big loss (over $1.6 million – ouch) selling so many items so far under cost. However, it was our mistake. We will be honoring all purchases that took place on 6pm.com during our mess up. We apologize to anyone that was confused and/or frustrated during out little hiccup and thank you all for being such great customers. We hope you continue to Shop. Save. Smile. at 6pm.com.

Nice job by 6pm.com to admit the mistake and take their medicine. The willingness to honor those discounted sales is admirable and more importantly a brand defining moment.

I love it when the folks from the C-Suite get down in the trenches. Zappos CEO Tony Hsieh (Shay) is never afraid to address an issue. Here is his update to the original blog post: {Endnote 131}

We have a pricing engine that runs and sets prices according to the rules it is given by business owners. Unfortunately, the way to input new rules into the current version of our pricing engine requires near-programmer skills to manipulate, and a few symbols were missed in the coding of a new rule, which resulted in items that were sold exclusively on 6pm.com to have a maximum price of $49.95. (Items that are sold on both 6pm.com and Zappos.com were not affected.)

We already had planned on improving our internal pricing engine so that it will have a much easier-to-use interface for our business owners. We are also planning on adding additional checks and balances to hopefully prevent this type of thing from happening again.

To those of you asking if anybody was fired, the answer is no, nobody was fired – this was a learning experience for all of us. Even though our terms and conditions state that we do not need to fulfill orders that are placed due to pricing

169

mistakes, and even though this mistake cost us over $1.6 million, we felt that the right thing to do for our customers was to eat the loss and fulfill all the orders that had been placed before we discovered the problem.

PS: To put an end to any further speculation about my tweet, I will also confirm that I did not, in fact, eat any ice cream on Sunday night.

[Make your ice cream a triple scoop Tony. Well deserved on how you handled this situation.]

3. Making good in response to the Snowpocalypse [PG #715]

Taken from a post by Axel Murillo {Endnote 132} of Worldwide Business Research USA LLC:

Like one of tens of thousands of people traveling this past holiday season, I had booked a JetBlue flight for the day after Christmas to spend quality time with friends and loved ones. However, Mother Nature had other plans. A storm that quickly produced between 12 and 32 inches of snow fell on many areas of the Northeast that eventually caused the cancellation of some 10,000 flights. It certainly earned its title as the "Snowpocalypse," or "Snowmaggeddon" of 2010.

[Editors Note: Axel's flight was canceled and rescheduled a total of four times. Each of his reschedules were done via Twitter.]

My trip to Austin eventually went off without too many more delays, once again letting me take for granted things like roomier leather seats on coach, and DirecTV for everyone. Since I pretty much only fly JetBlue these days, I tend to forget that other airlines don't offer what I've come to think of as common sense expectations.

A few days after my return to New York, along with all other passengers affected by the "Snowpocalypse," I received an email from Robin Hayes, Chief Commercial Officer for JetBlue Airways that partly read:

"As a token of our appreciation for your patience during last week's snowstorm when we canceled your flight, please accept 10,000 TrueBlue points which you can apply toward future travel to any JetBlue destination."

If I add those to my existing points, I got a free round trip ticket to Austin anytime! I'm more than satisfied; I am fairly star-struck by this rock-star quality treatment! By any conventional means, JetBlue has no responsibility to provide such perks to assuage climate disruptions. But the fact is that they did; that's what I call a phenomenal customer experience.

Marketing Lagniappe Takeaway: Be proactive when faced with service disruption. Great job by JetBlue to offer the complimentary TrueBlue points.

4. Who is this Gary character? [PG #170]

I went to see Gary Vaynerchuk speak at a MENG {Endnote 133} (Marketing Executives Networking Group) NJ Chapter event in Morristown, New Jersey. Gary was awesome in his typical "no holds barred" fashion. I came in with high expectations and he exceeded them.

He shared a recent example from his company WineLibrary.com. He recounted that a recent order was screwed up via FedEx, not WineLibrary's fault but that didn't matter to the customer. A Wine Library staffer drove the shipment down south three hours to the Jersey Shore and hand delivered it to the customer.

THE RESULT: That customer immediately reached out to his network over three or four tweets to laud WineLibrary.com and recommend them "hands down" over the competition.

[Note: Gary alluded that there might be some other 'branded acts of kindness' coming down the proverbial (New Jersey) turnpike. He talked about the next major snow storm and the possibility of shoveling the driveways of his best customers.

Imagine yourself as a customer and Gary shows up at your doorstep, shovel in hand. That's a purple goldfish I'd like to see.]

5. Sharpening the Scissors [PG #996]

Taken from a post {Endnote 134} by Forbes columnist Dean Crutchfield of The Caffeine Partnership:

Just recently I visited one of Sur La Table's stores in Manhattan with my entire set of Wüsthof knives in search of their door-buster deal of free blade sharpening. I brought in the lot, even the scissors, only to be informed by the assistant (and the small print) that the offer was for only two knives. I was already in the store, so blaming my reading glasses, as one does, I paid for all the knives (bar two) and left feeling duped and disgruntled.

Two days later, after returning home from picking up, I realized there were no scissors. I called, explained and received a very courteous reply that they do not sharpen scissors, and that my set had likely been misplaced so it was best for me to come back in and get a replacement pair free of charge, even though I did not have the receipt. From there, the experience was like floating on air. An absolute delight that led me to informing the management at the store and their headquarters that the whole shop experience was amazing.

Chapter 25

Lagniappe Category: Technology

"The most exciting breakthroughs of the 21st century will not occur because of technology but because of an expanding concept of what it means to be human."

- John Naisbitt

Technology is becoming a game changer in marketing. Let's look at three companies who are using RFID, QR Codes and computer chips to provide a little something extra for customers:

1. RFID + Ice Cream [PG #995]

Taken from a post by Matrix Product Development: {Endnote 135}

> Izzy's Ice Cream Cafe of St. Paul serves over 150 flavors of handmade ice cream and always keeps 32 flavors in the case on any given day. I talked with Jeff Sommers today and he is super passionate about his ice cream and providing great customer service to serve it up.
>
> ***Here's what was happening at Izzy's:***
>
> When customers came to his store, they wanted to taste their favorite ice cream flavor. Sometimes it was not yet available and so people would leave feeling disappointed. Some people would purchase a different flavor, but Jeff really wanted total customer satisfaction and he searched for a way to provide it.
>
> Finding a way to let the patron know when their favorite flavor was available, reducing disappointment, was a prime concern for Jeff. It was a problem he needed to solve right away. The day he found a RFID technology solution for that

173

problem was the day revenue increased. He had solved the problem and provided added value.

RFID tags identify each flavor when it is placed in the case ready to serve. The RFID system updates the inventory every three minutes so you can be sure your favorite flavor is there when you have a craving.

If you choose to be notified by email, you can sign up and let the system know what flavors you are looking for. There are options to be notified by Twitter updates and Facebook alerts as well. Just sign up for the updates.

The effort Jeff took to find a solution for his customer is remarkable. I find it one of the most unique ways of using RFID tagging technology and bringing top notch customer service to a business.

When owners like Jeff go out of the way to serve their customer, I believe it's a story worth telling over and over again.

2. QR Codes + Squid Ink [PG #808]

Submitted by Andrew Sweet. Andrew and I caught up at an advisory board meeting at Marist College. He mentioned an interesting use of QR Codes from Taranta and Chef Jose Duarte.

Andrew talked about a segment he watched on Channel 5 about the Peruvian inspired Italian restaurant in the North End of Boston. Taranta uses squid ink to place QR codes on plates featuring fresh locally sourced seafood. Diners can scan the code to visit a site called Trace and Trust. {Endnote 136} It allows you to track where and when your fish was caught.

TARANTA USES QR CODES TO STAND OUT IN A SEA OF SAMENESS

marketinglagniappe.com

Marketing Lagniappe Takeaway: Talk about a signature extra. This one is signed in squid ink. A clever use a hot button technology to highlight the fact you source fresh seafood from local fishermen.

3. A Chip and a Hockey Jersey [PG #953]
Submitted via e-mail by Lee Silverstein of Tampa Bay Job Coach:

> Not long after experiencing the joy of winning the Stanley Cup in 2004, the Tampa Bay Lightning and their fans experienced the frustration of a new ownership group that spent more time fighting amongst themselves then running the team.
>
> That all changed when in February 2010, a new ownership group, led by billionaire hedge-fund manager, Jeff Vinik purchased the team. Vinik vowed to build both a winning team, and a winning fan experience; he has definitely put his money where his mouth is. Over the summer the St. Pete Times Forum, home of the Lightning, underwent a $40m renovation, funded entirely by Vinik. Now almost completed, the renovation included:
>
> - All new cushioned seats with cup-holders
> - Remodeled luxury boxes
> - An outdoor party deck that overlooks the city

175

- Tesla coils that shoot real "lightning" when the team scores

The two biggest changes to the fan experience; however, were the addition of the world's biggest digital theater organ and a new program that rewards season-ticket holders. Located on the third level of the Forum, the Lightning removed about 500 seats (and the revenue associated with those seats) for the organ. The instrument sits on a raised platform called the organ loft and is surrounded by a bar.

The Lightning's new program for their season ticket-holders is the first of its kind in professional sports. All full season ticket holders received a home game jersey with their respective season ticket commitments. In addition to the sweater's distinct look, a microchip is inserted in the sleeve, thereby allowing season ticket holders to be identified at concession stands and merchandise shops throughout the St. Pete Times Forum. By scanning these embedded sleeves, fans receive a 25% discount on all concessions in the arena and a 35% discount on all merchandise purchased at the Times Forum during Lightning games.

To me, the biggest "Lagniappe" of all came when it was announced that Jeff Vinik and his wife, Penny will be donating more than $10 million through the Lightning Foundation to deserving community heroes and charity partners in Tampa Bay over the next five years. During each and every home game (41 games!), the Lightning Foundation will select and honor a Community Hero. Their heroic efforts will be celebrated by making a $50,000 contribution to an eligible 501(c)(3) organization that represents that Hero's cause.

Top 12 Key Takeaways

"Advice is like a tablet of aspirin.
It only works if you actually take it."
- David Murphy

Let us count the Top 12 most important takeaways from *What's Your Purple Goldfish?*:

#1. The Biggest Myth in Marketing

There is no such thing as meeting expectations. You either exceed them or you fall short.

#2. Choose Wisely

You can't be all things to all people. You only have two choices as a marketer: Create to spec and face being a commodity or set out to exceed expectations and become remarkable.

#3. Shareholders vs. Customers?

Business is about creating and keeping customers. Customer experience should be Priority #1 in your marketing. Stop focusing on the "two in the bush" (prospects) and take care of the one in your hand (customers).

#4. Value is the New Black

Don't compete on price. Cater to the 70% that buy based on value. Price is only relative to the value received.

#5. Phelps Corollary to the Pareto Principle

Traditional marketing is flawed. Eighty percent of your efforts will net 20% of your results. Focus on existing customers instead of the funnel by finding little extras that are tangible, valuable and talkable.

#6. Growth is Determined by Five Factors

The growth of your product or service is similar to that of a goldfish. Growth is determined by 5 factors: Size of the bowl (Market), # of other goldfish in the bowl (Competition), Quality of the water in the bowl (Business Environment / Economy), First 120 Days of Life (Start-up) and Genetic make-up (Differentiation). Assuming you've already been in business for four months, the only thing you can control is how you differentiate yourself.

#7. Purple Goldfish Strategy

Purple Goldfish Strategy is "differentiation via added value." Finding signature extras that help you stand out, improve customer experience, reduce attrition and drive positive word of mouth.

#8. Acts of Kindness

Think of lagniappe as an added branded act of kindness. A beacon or sign that shows you care. Marketing via G.L.U.E (giving little unexpected extras). A little something thrown in for good measure.

#9. Lagniappe Economy

There is a middle ground between a Market Economy (quid pro quo) and a Gift Economy (free). A lagniappe economy is where there is an exchange of goods and services for an exact value (market economy), plus a little unexpected extra that is given for good measure (gift economy).

#10. v4 Principle

V4 is when a consumer becomes a PROsumer. They stand up for a product or service and vouch for it, giving personal assurances to its value. As a marketer you need to figure out a way to make your product or service remark-able. Are you giving your customers something to talk, tweet, blog and post to Facebook about?

#11. Five Ingredients

There are 5 ingredients or R.U.L.E.S when creating a purple goldfish:

> **R**elevant - the extra should be of value to the recipient

> **U**nexpected - it should "surprise and delight"

> **L**imited - the extra should be something rare, hard to find or signature to your business

> **E**xpression - it should be a sign that you care

> **S**ticky - it should be memorable and talkable

#12. Value / Maintenance Matrix

The VM matrix calculates how a brand measures up on two important criteria: value and maintenance. The goal is to be seen as "high value" and "low maintenance" by your customers. There are 12 types of Purple Goldfish based on value and maintenance:

#1. **Throw-ins** (value)	#7. **Thank You** (maintenance)
#2. **In the Bag** (value)	#8. **Added Service** (maintenance)
#3. **Sampling** (value)	#9. **Convenience** (maintenance)
#4. **Impressions** (value)	#10. **Waiting** (maintenance)
#5. **Guarantees** (value)	#11. **Special Needs** (maintenance)
#6. **Pay it forward** (value)	#12. **Handling Mistakes** (maintenance)

Final Thoughts

I hope you enjoyed the book. I want to make five final points about marketing lagniappe.

You Can't Make Chicken Salad...

You can't make chicken salad out of chicken poop [apologies for using "poop" as I have four and five year old boys]. Creating a purple goldfish is not a substitute for having a strong product or service. Get the basics right before considering the little unexpected extras.

Authentic vs. Forced

A purple goldfish is a beacon. A small gift or offering that demonstrates you care. It needs to be done in an authentic way. If it comes across as forced or contrived, you'll eliminate all of the goodwill and negatively impact your product or service.

A Daily Regiment of Exercise vs. Liposuction

Marketing Lagniappe is not a quick fix or for those seeking immediate results. Translation: it's not liposuction. It's equivalent to working out every day. The results gradually build and improve over time.

It's a Commitment, Not a Campaign

A Purple Goldfish is different than a promotion or limited time offer. It's a feature that becomes embedded into the fabric of your product or service. Add one or a school of goldfish at your convenience, remove them at your peril.

Every Great Journey Begins With a Single Step

Start small when adding a signature extra and add gradually. The best brands are those who boast a whole school of purple goldfish.

Additional Inspiration and Further Reading

Looking for exemplary companies. Here are my Hall of Famers:

Class of 2010	Class of 2011	Class of 2012
DoubleTree	Trader Joe's	Mitchells
Stew Leonard's	Nordstrom	Pizza Shuttle
TD Bank	Starbucks	Besito
Southwest Airlines	Disney	IKEA
Five Guys	Four Seasons	Kiehl's
Zappos	JetBlue	Michael Lynne's
Lexus	Izzy's	Taranta
Kimpton Hotels	Amazon	L.L. Bean
AJ Bombers	Whole Foods	Zane's Cycles

Further reading on marketing and customer experience.

Books I would highly recommend:

Delivering Happiness by Tony Hsieh

Hug Your Customers by Jack Mitchell

The Next Evolution of Marketing by Bob Gilbreath

The Thank You Economy by Gary Vaynerchuk

The Experience Effect by Jim Joseph

Purple Cow by Seth Godin

Domino by Linda Ireland

My Story by Stew Leonard

FREE by Chris Anderson

Winning the Customer by Lou Imbriano

99.3 Random Acts of Marketing by Drew McLellan

Five Star Customer Service by Ted Coiné

The End of Business as Usual by Brian Solis

B-A-M by Barry Moltz

Killing Giants by Stephen Denny

Tipping Point by Malcolm Gladwell

The New Rules of Marketing & PR by David Meerman Scott

Endnotes

1. http://9inchmarketing.com/2008/12/21/the-gift/

2. http://www.drewsmarketingminute.com/2009/04/recency-where-is-the-lagniappe-in-your-marketing-stan-phelps.html

3. http://www.slideshare.net/9INCHMARKETING/marketing-lagniappe-in-search-of-your-purple-goldfish-2086426

4. http://9inchmarketing.com/2009/09/13/wells-fargos-marketing-lagniappe-gets-them-an-attaboy/

5. http://www.marketinglagniappe.com/blog/1001-examples-of-lagniappe/

6. https://www.wellsfargo.com/invest_relations/vision_values/5

7. http://www.marketinglagniappe.com/blog/

8. http://itunes.apple.com/us/podcast/marketing-lagniappe-the-purple/id360579251

9. http://www.ideafinder.com/history/inventors/mcconnell.htm

10. http://www.stacyssnacks.ca/English/stacy.html

11. http://www.ad-mkt-review.com/public_html/docs/fs157.html

12. http://buzzcanuck.typepad.com/agentwildfire/2006/01/top_11_killer_s.html

13. http://www.mediapost.com/publications/article/150041/

14. http://www.demandware.com/Demandware-Survey-Reveals-Web-Centric-Consumers-Have-Highly-Volatile-Brand-Loyalty/pr_2011_05_03,default,pg.html

15. https://freshbuzzmedia.com/2010/10/word-of-mouth-stats-to-know

16. http://www.slideshare.net/agentwildfire/agent-wildfire-cheat-sheet

17. http://www.tell3000.com/

18. http://www.youtube.com/watch?v=5_uSl6hlM7c

19. http://www.pmalink.com/?p=148

20. http://sethgodin.typepad.com/seths_blog/2010/02/once-in-a-lifetime.html

21. http://www.colorado.edu/studentgroups/libertarians/issues/friedman-soc-resp-business.html

22. http://www.thewisemarketer.com/features/read.asp?id=7

185

23. http://hbswk.hbs.edu/archive/5075.html

24. http://www.brandkeys.com/awards/

25. http://en.wikipedia.org/wiki/Pareto_principle

26. http://www.quotationspage.com/quote/1992.html

27. http://www.youtube.com/watch?v=3ed7B6ug-wk

28. http://news.bbc.co.uk/2/hi/uk_news/england/kent/7352909.stm

29. http://www.novareinna.com/festive/mardi.html

30. http://www.novareinna.com/festive/mardi.html

31. http://www.sethgodin.com/purple/

32. http://www.fastcompany.com/magazine/67/purplecow.html

33. http://bobhebertonline.com/2011/08/book-review-purple-cow-transform-your-business-by-being-remarkable-by-seth-godin/

34. http://www.marketingpilgrim.com/2010/01/cup-of-joe-give-me-a-smart-phone-with-pink-purple-stripes.html

35. http://www.blueoceanstrategy.com/abo/what_is_bos.html

36. https://secure.digitalcontentcenter.com/shop/392120/viewcart/?AddProduct=8200

37. http://www.merriam-webster.com/dictionary/lagniappe

38. http://docsouth.unc.edu/southlit/twainlife/twainnoil.html

39. http://www.todayifoundout.com/index.php/2010/09/why-a-bakers-dozen-is-13-instead-of-12/

40. http://blogs.hbr.org/cs/2011/04/coca-colas_marketing_shift_fro.html

41. http://www.rickliebling.com/2009/11/24/marketing-lagniappe-with-a-side-of-curly-fries/

42. http://mylifeinquotes.posterous.com/

43. http://www.amazon.com/How-Be-Like-Walt-Capturing/dp/0757302319

44. http://www.marketinglagniappe.com/blog/2010/08/12/walter-elias-disney-and-the-plus-factor/

45. http://en.wikipedia.org/wiki/Gift_economy

46. http://socialmediamediasres.wordpress.com/2011/02/16/social-media-is-like-beer-buying-the-gift-economy-in-social-media/

47. http://www.marketinglagniappe.com/blog/2010/12/26/what-is-a-purple-goldfish-its-a-beacon/

186

48. http://www.marketinglagniappe.com/blog/1001-examples-of-lagniappe/

49. http://www.marketinglagniappe.com/blog/2009/11/29/doubletree-hotels-the-1st-purple-goldfish-project-hall-of-famer/

50.http://doubletree.hilton.com/en/dt/promotions/dt_cookie/index.jhtml;jsessionid=YW32IHJPP2O
W4CSGBJT222Q

51. http://www.usatoday.com/travel/columnist/baskas/2010-01-13-unusual-airport-freebies_N.htm

52. http://www.nytimes.com/2010/01/12/business/12cookies.html

53. http://en.wikipedia.org/wiki/The_Tipping_Point

54. http://bit.ly/tE7b62

55. http://www.inc.com/magazine/20100401/jerry-murrell-five-guys-burgers-and-fries.html

56. http://www.sportbikes.net/archives/forums/showthread.php?t=8996

57. http://www.kellerfay.com/wp-content/uploads/2011/01/WordofMouthPolitics.pdf

58. http://www.altimetergroup.com/about/team/brian-solis

59. http://www.briansolis.com/2009/04/can-statusphere-save-journalism/

60. http://www.marketinglagniappe.com/blog/2010/05/27/customer-experience-is-the-ultimate-differentiator/

61. http://stellaservice.com/

62. http://www.lyricsfreak.com/b/bonnie+raitt/something+to+talk+about_20022654.html

63. http://www.marketinglagniappe.com/blog/2010/01/14/bmw-drives-into-the-purplegoldfishproject-at-150/

64. http://forums.nasioc.com/forums/showthread.php?t=1348892

65. http://www.tiffany.com/Expertise/Diamond/certification/engraving_and_cleaning.aspx

66. http://adage.com/article/cmo-strategy/marketing-effective-word-mouth-disrupts-schemas/141734/

67. http://www.secret.com/secret-clinical-strength.aspx

68. http://klm.prezly.com/klm-surprises-customers

69. http://www.marketinglagniappe.com/blog/2009/12/26/5-main-ingredients-of-lagniappe/

70. http://www.facebook.com/note.php?note_id=92123312218

71. http://www.urbanspoon.com/r/201/1422800/restaurant/Long-Island/Besito-Huntington

187

72. http://cruises.about.com/od/cruisenews/a/050209carnival.htm

73. http://www.drewsmarketingminute.com/2010/11/creating-love-affairs-you-cant-buy-their-love.html

74. http://www.tell3000.com/

75. http://onmilwaukee.com/dining/wineanddine/articles/pizzashuttlepizza.html

76. http://consumerist.com/2010/12/hotel-washes-every-coin-they-get-as-courtesy-for-guests.html

77. http://www.forbes.com/forbes/2004/0621/068_print.html

78. http://www.thefreedictionary.com/lagniappe

79. http://www.southwest.com/html/cs/landing/bags_flyfree.html

80. http://www.tripadvisor.com/ShowUserReviews-g60628-d114056-r7841247-Four_Seasons_Resort_Lana_i_The_Lodge_at_Koele-Lanai_City_Lanai_Hawaii.html

81. http://www.beyondphilosophy.com/thought-leadership/blog/singapore-aiport-slides-towards-memorable-customer-experience

82. http://www.lvrj.com/neon/stripsteak-s-careful-preparation-shows-even-simple-things-perfectly-prepared-112707359.html?ref=359

83. http://www.allstatenewsroom.com/releases/6507f11e-eeac-413e-a441-7d24547dece5?mode=print

84. http://nymag.com/listings/bar/alligator_lounge/

85. http://www.flipthefunnelnow.com/

86. http://www.t-shirtforums.com/general-t-shirt-selling-discussion/t21752-12.html

87. http://www.charlotteobserver.com/

88. http://blog.stellaservice.com/2010/06/14/have-you-seen-any-purple-goldfish-lately/

89. http://www.mltennis.com/

90. http://www.adweek.com/

91. http://www.marketinglagniappe.com/blog/2010/07/18/purple-goldfish-meng-webinar/

92. http://beauty.thefuntimesguide.com/2007/09/kiehls_free_samples.php

93. http://www.sundoginteractive.com/sunblog/posts/the-brand-experience-and-the-peak-end-rule

94. http://www.forbes.com/sites/deancrutchfield/2011/12/19/i-experience-therefore-i-shop/

95. http://www.lostremote.com/2010/01/15/social-media-powers-local-word-of-mouth-marketing/

96. http://www.exit133.com/5551/hotel-murano-6-in-conde-nast-readers

97. http://blogs.wsj.com/middleseat/2009/12/11/clooneys-up-in-the-air-is-it-about-miles-or-mileage/

98. http://www.businessvoice.com/blog/are-you-delivering-cold-drinks/

99. http://www.louimbriano.com/2011/03/24/its-universal-theyre-trying-harder/

100. http://alaskanlibrarian.wordpress.com/2008/08/25/jansport-delivers/

101. http://lamenta3.disavian.net/2009/02/return-of-the-backpack/

102.http://www.netpromoter.com/netpromoter_community/blogs/conference_ny_2010/2010/02/0
2/bliss-zane-s-cycles-southwest-usaa-driving-extreme-loyalty

103. http://www.qsrmagazine.com/news/coffee-bean-tea-leaf-run-promotion-troops

104. http://www.gaspedal.com/

105. http://disneyparks.disney.go.com/

106. http://thankyoueconomybook.com/

107. http://www.1to1media.com/weblog/2011/05/customer_experience_balancing.html

108. http://businessnetworking.com/the-friendly-skies-are-back/

109. http://www.kristinaevey.com/customer-satisfaction/excellent-customer-service-is-the-best-
prescription/

110. http://theexperiencefactor.com/whats-your-purple-goldfish/795/

111. http://directmag.com/online/marketing_workers_paradise/

112. http://posborne1.wordpress.com/2009/09/30/simply-great-service-zappos/

113 http://www.upyourservice.com/learning-library/customer-service-innovation/find-a-do-your-
own-thing

114.http://www.customerthink.com/blog/safelite_repairs_safelite_replace_safelite_does_a_little_ex
tra

115. http://jimjosephexp.blogspot.com/

116. http://www.seriouseats.com/

117. http://www.upyourservice.com/

118.http://www.customerthink.com/blog/great_wolf_lodge_takes_a_proactive_approach_to_service
_around_peak_times

119. http://neonlimelight.com/2010/07/08/lady-gaga-sends-fans-water-and-pizza-to-ease-today-show-concert-camp-out/

120. http://www.mediapost.com/publications/article/128180/

121. http://www.lexusofnorthmiami.com/WebSiteSurvey

122. http://changingwinds.wordpress.com/2011/02/10/how-to-blow-away-the-competition-through-leadership-why-td-bank-kicks-butt/

123. http://studenthousingguy.blogspot.com/2010/06/what-is-your-purple-goldfish.html

124. http://www.marketinglagniappe.com/blog/free-ebook/

125. http://tysullivan.blogspot.com/2010/12/tales-of-heart-from-twitterville.html

126. http://theexperiencefactor.com/whats-your-purple-goldfish/795/

127. http://www.nytimes.com/2011/01/11/business/11allergy.html?_r=1&emc=eta1

128. http://saltandpeppergroup.com/blog/2010/12/5-reasons-the-rainforest-cafe-saved-the-day/

129.http://www.amazon.com/Customer-Love-Great-Stories-Service/dp/1608100189/ref=sr_1_2?s=books&ie=UTF8&qid=1295495369&sr=1-2

130. http://blogs.zappos.com/blogs/inside-zappos/2010/05/21/6pm-com-pricing-mistake

131. http://blogs.zappos.com/blogs/inside-zappos/2010/05/21/6pm-com-pricing-mistake

132. http://www.theetailblog.com/customer-experience/one-customers-jetblue-customer-experience/

133. http://www.mengonline.com/index.jspa

134. http://www.forbes.com/sites/deancrutchfield/2011/12/19/i-experience-therefore-i-shop/

135. http://matrixpd.com/index.php/blog/11-food-processing/74-rfid-technology-increases-revenue-for-izzys.html

About the Author

Stan Phelps is Chief Solutions Officer at Synergy Events [synergyevents.com]. Founded in 1992, Synergy is an award winning experiential marketing agency. At Synergy Stan takes a wide look at marketing with the premise of finding unique ways to engage customers. He creates signature experiences that accelerate business results.

Stan believes the longest and hardest nine inches in marketing is the distance between the brain and the heart of a customer. He's committed to exploring the concept of marketing lagniappe. *What's Your Purple Goldfish?* is the first book in a trilogy on the subject.

The second book, *What's Your Green Goldfish?* will take a look a the signature extras a business provides to their employees to improve morale, reduce attrition and create a dynamic culture. The final installment will be *What's Your Golden Goldfish?* It will focus on the extras you provide for both your top 20% of customers and top 20% of employees.

Stan received a BS in marketing from Marist College and a JD/MBA from Villanova University. He lives in Cary, NC with his wife Jennifer, their two boys Thomas & James and a Glen of Imaal Terrier named MacMurphy.

Twitter: @9INCHmarketing

Email: stan@9inchmarketing.com

Blog: 9inchmarketing.com

LAGNIAPPE FOR BOOK PURCHASERS

Thanks for purchasing *What's Your Purple Goldfish?* One cannot write a book about lagniappe without throwing in a signature added value or two for good measure.

Limited Collector's Edition* - I've created a set of eight inspirational cards that highlight the key concepts in the book. Send me an e-mail with your address and proof of purchase (picture of you holding the book, Amazon receipt or screenshot of your receipt) and I'll mail you the set gratis. My e-mail is stan@9inchmarketing.com.

* Limited run of 1,000